GW01466085

English & French
DINKY TOYS
Price Guide
2nd Edition

Publisher & Editor: Simon Epton

Copyright © Toy Price Guide

ISBN 978-0-9565015-3-0

Designed in the UK by KK Design Services

Printed in the UK by Buxton Press

Published in the UK by the Toy Price Guide

Pictures by the author unless stated

Front cover images:
28 Series ENSIGN Delivery Van (1st type)
522 Big Bedford , cerise & cream version
French Dinky 1406 Renault Sinpar

Registered Address:
Toy Price Guide, Orchard House, North End Lane, Fulbeck, Grantham, Lincs, NG32 3JR
Tel 01400 279177

Contents

Our guide lists 1000 models together with the many colour & packaging variations released during 1934-1979. Gift sets can be found at the end of each section

07 Editors Welcome

08 Current market

09 Price Guide Calculator & Abbreviations

14 The History of Dinky Toys

UK Made Dinky Toys

16 Cars – Saloon, Rally & Racing

38 Caravans

38 Aircraft

45 Boats, Ships & Hovercraft

47 Bus & Coach

51 Taxi

52 Emergency - Ambulance

53 Emergency - Fire

54 Emergency – Police

57 Farm

62 Lorries, Vans & Commercials

86 Construction

88 Military

93 Motorcycles

94 TV & Film

SPECIAL THANKS

The Toy Price Guide is committed to working with quality toy specialists whose services we recommend to collectors; in particular we would like to thank our advertisers for their support (see below) together with Wallis & Wallis, Vectis, Warwick & Warwick, DJ Auctions & Special Auction Services for providing the photographs within this guide.

ADVERTISING INDEX

Andrew Clark 50

Astons Toy Auctions 13

Barry Potter 28

DJ Auctions 10, 76, 119

Miniature Autoworld 10

Richardsons 13

Special Auction Services 132

Toyman Displays 6

Wallis & Wallis 2

Warwick & Warwick 131

97 Railway

101 Action Kits

102 Accessory Sets

103 Dublo

French Made Dinky

104 Cars

116 Aircraft

118 Ships

118 Bus & Coach

120 Emergency

120 Farm

121 Lorries, Vans & Commercials

126 Construction

127 Military

129 Railway

CONTACT US

Editor & Publisher - Simon Epton info@toypriceguide.co.uk

To become a Trade Stockist email us on info@toypriceguide.co.uk

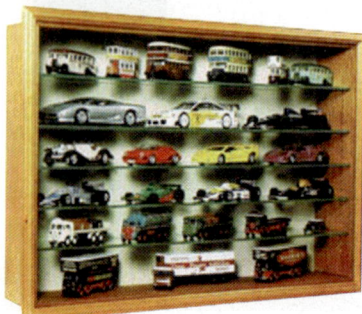

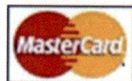

EDITORS WELCOME

Thank you to everyone who purchased our first Dinky Toys (75th Anniversary) Price Guide, due to overwhelming demand we sold out after only 10 months forcing us to bring the 2nd edition out much earlier than planned.

Included in this edition is a comprehensive section dedicated to French Dinky Toys which are becoming increasingly popular with UK collectors resulting in many now turning up in auction rooms around the country enabling us to provide an accurate price guide. Once again I have teamed up with the leading collecting experts and special UK toy auction houses to bring you this price guide.

Our Dinky guide is the ONLY current price guide dedicated to Dinky Toys and has been compiled using our archive of original catalogues, conversations with dealers, access to private collections together with several decades spent gathering content at collector's fairs, traditional auction salerooms and more recently online auctions.

Where possible 'real prices' have been used for individual items, these exclude commission and are based on items sold in 2009/10. For rarer items that seldom come up for sale we have published the date last sold. As prices vary we recommend allowing a 10% margin of error as well as taking into consideration the auctioneer's commission (generally 10-15%). We are always looking out for fresh information so if you know of any colour, packaging, wheel, seat or decal variations not listed we ask you to make us aware of them. Details of how to contact us appear on page 3 or you can get in touch via our website using the 'contact us' page.

Happy Collecting!
Simon Epton

ABOUT THE TOY PRICE GUIDE

We are a unique publishing company with a keen interest in the history of toys and are dedicated to building a range of special interest Toy & Childhood Memorabilia publications, both in print form and online, enabling collectors or those selling collectables to identify the latest market value for their collection.

We currently have 7 other guides available; Action Man (£4.99), Britains Toys 2nd Edition (£9.99) and Classic TV & Film Toys (£6.99), Hornby Trains (£7.99), Corgi Toys (£9.99) & Tri-ang Toys (£8.99)

Special Auction Services Announcement
Please note Special Auction Services have a new address as follows:
81 Greenham Park, Newbury RG19 6HW   Tel: 0118 971 2949

Collect for pleasure not for profit are always our words of advice to anyone new looking to build a collection, however it is always reassuring to hear your collection is appreciating in value. In spite of the well documented financial problems both at home and abroad demand and prices remain strong with many record prices reached for individual mint boxed items. Additionally this does not include items sold online as Buy It Now items which regularly sell for even higher prices.

Good prices are still emerging from UK auction houses; DJ auctions September 2010 all Dinky sale a mint boxed pre-war No.48 Filling & Service Station made £540, an unboxed 25t Flat Truck & Trailer (blue) made a record £300, 107 Sunbeam Alpine (light blue) £200, 482 DINKY TOYS livery Bedford van another record at £220, WEETABIX Guy van £2500 with the star of the show being a 934 blue version Leyland Octopus realising £3000. Special Auction Services October 2010 sale included five 1st type 28 Series Vans of which the Kodak and Ensign Camera livery versions realised £1500 each, also sold separately was the empty box for the vans in fair condition and missing dividers realising an amazing £800. Wallis & Wallis sales throughout the year included a rare French Dinky Trade Pack containing 6 Karts realising £390, double estimate and previous best prices and a 989 U.S. issue Auto-Transporters Car Carrier in the rare yellow version sold for £560. Chris Aston of Aston's also commented that as well as fine condition boxed Dinky at the lower quality end large lots containing poor condition dinky (suitable for restoration) is increasingly popular.

As reported in the last guide more and more of the Dinky are going to Holland, Belgium, France, Australia, New Zealand, Canada and the USA, with dealers reporting difficulty finding quality toys to sell. So these factors can only feed the belief that values will continue on their upward trend for a while yet, though prices for average condition models appear to be off their peak. This means it's still a rosy time to collect Dinky Toys.

In this 2nd Edition we cover both English and French Dinky Toys together with models made for Export. As before we include pre-production samples, previously unrecorded colour variations and wherever possible we describe box type...

In most instances we show one price, in the case of scarce models/sets this is the most recent price achieved, for more popular models we take an average price. Where we include a price range (£90-110) this is likely to be an estimate as it has not recently been sold or perhaps sold with widely varying prices. All prices exclude buyer's commission so we recommend collectors allow a 10-20% margin of error to allow for this.

To establish the value of a particular model/box we have produced a Price Calculator on the following page, however it is always worth remembering the value of toys, particularly those sold via auctions, is dependent on 2 buyers wanting the same item so it should be used as an estimate only.

Disclaimer

Guide prices quoted are not intended to represent the price a dealer will offer it for sale, as the dealer more often is carrying expenses to offer customers a quality and reliable collecting service, which costs money to maintain. The price guide information does not constitute, nor should it be construed as, financial advice for investment purposes and as it states should be used as a guide only. The publisher, its agents and contributors shall not be liable for any loss or damage whatsoever arising as a result of reliance on any information contained within this guide.

This publication has been compiled solely for use as a reference guide. Whilst every care has been taken in compiling the guide the publisher cannot accept any responsibility whatsoever for errors and omissions or any financial loss, which may occur, as a result of its use.

Prices correct at the time of going to press on 1st July 2009

The guide price is based on mint/nr mint boxed items sold in 2009 and does not include auction house commission or P&P. Price depends on an items quality and packaging; items with play wear or missing packaging are in most instances worth only a fraction of the mint-boxed price. The scale below may help collectors apply values to their own collection:

For models and/or boxes compare the condition against the guide below for an estimated market value:

Model Value Calculator

Mint – perfect ex-shop condition 45%
Excellent – minor imperfections almost perfect 30-40%
Good – light playwear/minor paint chipping 20-30%
Average – obvious playwear with minor damage 10-20%
Poor – heavily play worn & damaged 1-10%
Repaint 10%

Box Value Calculator

Mint – perfect ex-shop condition 55%
Excellent – minor imperfections almost perfect 30-40%
Good – creasing, very light marks 20-30%
Average – slight tears, heavy creasing, and graffiti 10-20%
Poor – badly torn, very grubby, heavy graffiti 1-10%
Replacement box 5-10%

Example; Based on the popular 982 Pullmore Transporter (Price Guide £120) in excellent condition (x 30%) the model has a value nearing £36; if it comes in a torn (poor) box (x 10%) the box value is £12. Added together the model and box in this condition would be worth around £48.

For early models supplied to retailers in trade boxes/issued, regarded as unboxed, double the model value calculator and ignore the box calculator completely. Therefore if the model condition is excellent it is calculated at 60-80% of the quoted price guide.

TERMS OF REFERENCE & ABBREVIATIONS

The following abbreviations have been used to describe the condition and price of toys:

MIB	Mint in original Box	**PO**	Post Office
AA	Automobile Association	**U/B**	Unboxed
Ex	Excellent condition	**VW**	Volkswagen
RAC	Royal Automobile Club	**NPA**	No price available
VG	Very good condition	**RN**	Rally/Race Number

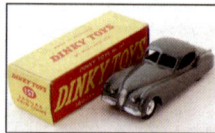

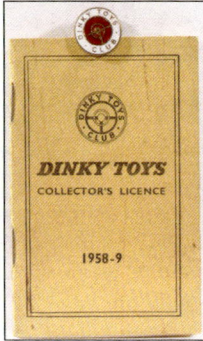

Dinky Toys collectors license & club lapel badge (1958-59), excellent condition.
Sold for £70 DJ Auctions

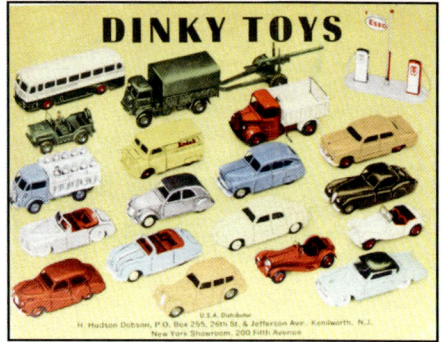

1955 US 32-page Catalogue for Hudson Dobson, excellent. Sold for £50 DJ Auctions

501 Foden Type1 Diesel 8 Wheel Wagon, brown, silver flash, no hook, brown hubs, nr mint in excellent brown box. Sold for £460 DJ Auctions

232 Alfa Romeo, red, RN8, mint in a rare blister card pack. Sold for £100 Wallis & Wallis

108 MG Midget, competition finish, red, tan seats, driver, red ridged hubs, RN24, mint in a crushed yellow box with correct colour spot.
Sold for £160 DJ Auctions

161 Austin Somerset Saloon, 2-tone yellow & red, red ridged hubs, near mint in crushed yellow box with correct colour spot. Sold for £320 DJ Auctions

South African issue 184 Volvo 122S, turquoise with white interior, good condition, unboxed. Sold for £220 Special Auction Services

169 Studebaker Golden Hawk, green/cream, spun hubs, VG in VG red/yellow box. Sold for £85 Special Auction Services

254 Austin Taxi, black, spun hubs, mint in excellent yellow box with correct colour spot. Sold for £170 DJ Auctions

998 Bristol Britannia CANADIAN PACIFIC Airliner, red stripe window panels, mint in excellent early style blue/white striped box. Sold for £75 Special Auction Services

718 Hawker Hurricane mint bubble pack complete with instruction leaflet. Sold for £65 Special Auction Services

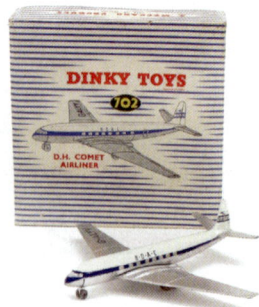

702 BOAC DH Comet Airliner, mint in excellent box complete with packing piece. Sold for £110 Special Auction Services

DINKY TOYS HISTORY

PRE-WAR
In 1931 Meccano issued a range of Modelled Miniatures railway track workers, passengers, station staff and other trackside accessories to complement their O gauge Hornby Railways system. In December 1933 six model cars were advertised in Meccano Magazine, and following the popularity prompted Frank Hornby, in 1934, to expand the range to include die-cast model ships and aeroplanes, and it was here Meccano Dinky Toys where christened.

Prior to the outbreak of World War II Dinky Toys were cast from an impure alloy, believed to be lead from Hornby Train production along with lead sack ties from the factory finding their way into the metal, and corrupting it, leading to many models suffering badly from fatique, making mint examples extremely rare and highly valued.

The first individually available model was the 23a Sports Car based on an early MG and by December 1935 the Dinky range had grown to include about 200 different products, including the 30 Series of cars featuring a more accurate likeness to the real thing and the 28 Series of delivery vans with personalised liveries of popular companies of thed ay. The first cars and commercial models were generally supplied to retailers in trade packs of 6 and only became available in individual boxes from 1952.

In the early Dinky years aeroplanes and ships formed a considerable part of the output of the Binns Road factory alongside models of cars and vans. Both civilian and military aircraft were produced and the Spitfire model was generously sold in a special presentation box between 1939 and 1941 as part of The Spitfire Fund to raise money for the production of real Spitfires. Although the production of aircraft models continued after the war, the heyday of Dinky ships was 1934-39.

During the Second World War production halted at the Binns Road factory in Liverpool and was given over to the Allied War effort.

POST-WAR
In the late 1940's production resumed with the first significant release being the 40 Series of British Saloon Cars which introduced greater casting accuracy than earlier models, manufactured from a better quality alloy, meaning higher survival rates and although originally sold from trade packs of six, early dual numbered boxes were introduced allowing stock models to make way for later renumbered versions. These boxes are highly prized today as very limited numbers were produced. Two-tone paintwork in conjunction with renumbering in 1954 saw models sold in boxes with dual spots on the end flaps, these to command premium prices. Most of the models were in a scale of approximately 1:48, which corresponding with O gauge railway sets, but buses and lorries were scaled down further so that they were about 4 inches long.

As part of the post-war development and range expansion, in 1947 Meccano Ltd introduced the SUPERTOYS series of 1:48 model lorries. To many collectors these are the most desirable Dinky Toys, and big premiums are paid for rare issues and unusual variations. The company continued producing these well detailed commercials through the 1950s, however even as the range became more sophisticated throughout the 1950s due to the lack of any real competition development of the models was perhaps slower than it could have been. This all changed in July 1956 when Mettoy introduced the Corgi range with the clear plastic windows. For the first time Dinky Toys had a direct competitor which lead to models releases with more sophisticated features.

In 1964 Tri-ang took over the parent Meccano company including Hornby trains and the Meccano construction range. Since Dinky Toys were more popular than Tri-ang's Spot-On model range, the latter were phased out in 1967 and a few cars originally designed for Spot-On were made in Hong Kong and marketed as Dinky Toys. From this point Dinky used the 1:42 scale for many of the English made cars and trucks, although the French factory stuck to the 1:43 scale, already popular in Europe.

In 1968 U.S. toymaker Mattel introduced Hot Wheels to the UK market providing children with heightened play value. In an attempt to remain No.1 in this competitive market the company made innovative changes including being the first to introduce four opening doors, retractable aerials, Speedwheels, metallic paint, and jewelled headlights. These models proved expensive to manufacture and prices could only be kept down if quantities were sufficiently high enough, sadly lower production volumes, changing fashions in the toy industry, international competition, Trade Union practices and the switch to cheap labour in low wage countries meant the days of British made Dinky Toys were numbered, and after attempts to simplify products to save costs, the Binns Road factory in Liverpool closed its doors in November 1979.

The Dinky trade-name changed hands many times before ending up as part of Matchbox International Ltd. in 1987, which saw the introduction of the Matchbox 'Dinky Collection' in 1988 designed for adult collectors. In 1992 TYCO acquired Matchbox Universal including the Dinky brand name, then in 1998 Mattel bought the Matchbox (including Dinky) brand announcing that new model cars would be launched as 'Dinky Toys. However no new "dedicated"

Dinky castings have been created in the Mattel era since Matchbox Collectibles was shut down in 2000, the company focussing on the Hot Wheels range instead.

DINKY ABROAD

France - In 1912 Frank Hornby set up a Paris office to import Meccano into France and by 1921 sales proved so successful that production of Meccano began in Paris at a new factory on Rue Rebeval, with a second plant opening in 1929 at Bobigny, where production of the Dinky Toys range would be based. Production in the early days was mainly model ships and aeroplanes, with vehicles gradually increasing in number. During WWII Meccano's French factories were commandered by the Germans for use in the Nazi war effort and also providing model vehicles for German toy company Marklin. Immediately after the war material shortages meant early post-war models had metal wheels due to Nazi activity cutting off supplies of rubber to France, rubber tyres were not fitted again until 1950. In 1951 the old factory at Rue Rebeval closed and Dinky Toys production was now solely based at Bobigny.

By the mid 1950s French Dinky Toys styling begun to move away from British models to concentrate on French and American motor manufacturers, the latter made popular by Hollywood movie stars filming and holidaying on the Riviera. By the 1960s virtually no crossover of products existed between the two countries resulting in an interesting range that complemented the better known UK models. The vast majority of the French Dinky Toys were only available in the home market although a few models did make it across the English Channel. In 1970 the Bobigny factory closed with production moving to Calais where the range continued to be manufactured until closure in 1971, though Spanish company Pilen produced some models which were originally sold as French Dinky Toys until the end of the decade.

South Africa - Meccano Ltd exported Dinky Toys to many of Britains old colonies relatively cheaply due to commonwealth trade agreements, with South Africa one of its biggest customers. In 1961 South Africa's withdrawl from the Commonwealth saw a luxury goods import tax imposed, making Dinky Toys very expensive and loss making for Meccano Ltd. so in 1962 the company began shipping parts to South Africa where models were assembled and painted locally as the import of unfinished goods was not subject to import tax. These models were sold in South Africa between 1962-63 and only one batch of each model is thought to have been produced, making South African Dinky Toys very rare. In 1966
South Africa also imported Dinky Toy parts from the French factory with six models assembled and painted locally. Distinguishing features of South African Dinky Toys are:
- Colours different from those on the same models assembled in the UK.
- Boxes with Afrikaan lettering and "Printed in South Africa" on the side.
- Gloss finish base plates compared to matt black base plates for UK models.

Hong Kong - Between 1965-67 six models were produced for Dinky Toys in Hong Kong for the US market. Originally intended to be produced as a part of the Spot-On range by Tri-ang the new owners decided re-brand them as Dinky Toys. In 1978/9 production of Dinky Toys in Hong Kong was tried again. These were poor quality models compared to earlier Dinky's, and were an attempt to cut production costs with the impending closure of the Binns Road Factory. The last new Meccano made Dinky Toys were produced in Hong Kong, and the Mk2 Ford Granada and Steed's Jaguar from the New Avengers TV series only exist as pre production samples, which are now amongst the most desirable of all Dinky Toys.

DINKY DUBLO

In December 1957 Meccano Ltd introduced the Dublo Dinky range of models in 1:76 scale, designed to be used with the Hornby Dublo railway system and very cheap to produce having a one piece die-cast metal body, baseplate and plastic wheels. It also meant Dinky were able to compete in the small scale toy car market dominated at the time by Lesney's Matchbox range. Although 14 models appeared in the range they met with limited success and a comparison of the Ford Prefect with the corresponding Matchbox model will go some way towards understanding why the Dublo Dinky range suffered from low sales. The first models were withdrawn in September 1959 with one only having been on sale for 18 months. Further models were withdrawn in October 1960, April 1962 and April 1964 until in December 1964 those models that remained were taken off the shelf seven years after Dublo Dinky Toys were introduced. Models were fitted with either smooth grey or grey & black knobbly plastic wheels, and values remain the same regardless of wheel type unless stated.

SMALL SCALE

In 1968, four years after Dublo's retirement another series of small scale models was introduced to a similar scale as the Matchbox range at 1:65. Mini-Dinky Toys, as the range was called, were of a high quality and featured opening bonnets, doors and boots and were produced in Hong Kong and Holland, with some construction models designed in Italy by Mercury to a 1:130 scale. In a bid to make this series stand out in toy shops each model was supplied in a plastic garage, complete with opening door, rather than the usual cardboard box. This novel feature was not enough to help sales as they now had to compete with Mattel's revolutionary Hot Wheels range, which ultimately signalled the end for Dinky's small scale cars.

The very first Dinky Toy to be produced 22a HORNBY SERIES Modelled Miniatures Open Sports Car, blue body, red seats, lead windscreen, VG unboxed. Sold for £190 Wallis & Wallis

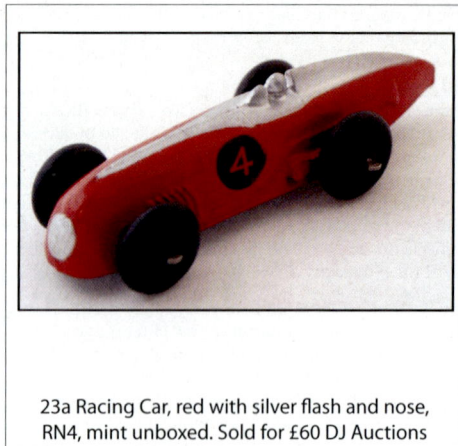

23a Racing Car, red with silver flash and nose, RN4, mint unboxed. Sold for £60 DJ Auctions

CARS

Ref.	First Issued	Model	TPG
22a	1933	**Sports Car,** open top, HORNBY SERIES cast inside, metal wheels. Unboxed	
		Grey	£700
		Red, broken windscreen	£110
		Cream. Sold in 2004	£1,300
		Blue	£350
		Green	£300-400
		Orange	£400
22b	1933	**Sports Coupe,** closed roof version, HORNBY SERIES cast inside, metal wheels. Unboxed	
		Red	£580
		Yellow	£480
		Orange	£440
		Blue	£380
22g	1935	**Streamline Tourer,** white rubber tyres. Unboxed	
		Cream	£100
		Green	£240
		Red	£130
		Maroon	£90
		Blue	£100
		Turquoise	£100
		Black	£130
22h	1935	**Streamlined Saloon,** no steering wheel. Unboxed	
		Lt Blue	£70
		Violet blue	£110
		Maroon	£110
		Cream	£70
		Red	£120
23a	1935	**Racing Car,** 1st type casting, with or without driver, white rubber tyres. Unboxed	
		Yellow/blue, driver, race number 1	£360
		Orange, no driver	£360
		Red, driver	£120
		Red/cream, driver	£110
		Cream/green, driver (play wear)	£80
23a	1946	**Racing Car,** 2nd type casting, driver, with or without race number. Unboxed	£60-70
		Green/cream striped version	£260
		Red/cream	£100
		Supplied to retailers in trade boxes of 6. Price for trade box with 1 model	£90

23c Mercedes Benz Racing Car, saxe blue, silver trim, tan driver, black ridged hubs, herringbone tyres, RN1, mint unboxed. Sold for £65 DJ Auctions

155 Ford Anglia, turquoise, excellent in creased and grubby box.
Sold for £65 Special Auction Services

23b	1935	**Hotchkiss Racing Car,** cream, blue, green, orange & yellow versions. Unboxed	£60-70
23b	1946	**Hotchkiss Racing Car,** race number 5, red & silver versions. Unboxed	£50-60
23c	1936	**Mercedes Benz Racing Car,** driver, race numbers on some, green, silver, blue, red & yellow versions. Unboxed	£40-50
23c	1946	**Mercedes Benz Racing Car,** with driver, various race numbers, blue & silver versions. Unboxed	£35-45
23d	1936	**Auto-Union Racing Car,** with or without driver, red, yellow, lt. green, silver & lt blue versions. Unboxed	£70-80
		Dark green version	£150
23d	1946	**Auto-Union Racing Car,** with or without driver, red or silver versions. Unboxed.	£50-60
23e	1935	**Speed of the Wind Racing Car,** yellow, red, blue, green or silver versions. Unboxed.	£50-60
23f	1952	**Alfa Romeo Racing Car** (renumbered 232), race no.8, red. Yellow picture box	£90
23g	1952	**Cooper Bristol Racing Car** (renumbered 233), race no.6, green. Yellow picture box	£100
23h	1953	**Ferrari Racing Car** (renumbered 234), race no.5, blue. Yellow picture box	£90
23j	1953	**HWM Racing Car** (renumbered 235), race no.7, green. Yellow picture box	£80
23k	1953	**Talbot Lago Racing Car** (renumbered 230), race no.4, blue. Yellow picture box	£85
23m	1938	**Thunderbolt Speed Car,** Union Jack decals. Unboxed	
		Green	£100
		Red	£140
		Silver, supplied in blue printed box	£180
23n	1953	**Maserati Racing Car** (renumbered 231), race no.9, red. Yellow picture box	£90
23p	1939	**Gardner's MG Record Car,** green, MG & Union Jack decals.	
		White side flash. Yellow box dated 9.39	£500
		No side flash. Unboxed	£80
23s	1938	**Streamlined Racing Car,** lead cast, orange, red, green, silver or blue. Unboxed	£30-40
		Supplied to retailers in trade boxes of 4. Price for a complete trade box	£130
23s	1948	**Streamlined Racing Car,** diecast (renumbered 222) in red, blue, orange, green or silver. Unboxed	£30-40
24b	1934	**Limousine,** maroon, blue & cream versions. Unboxed	£120-140
24c	1934	**Town Sedan.** Unboxed	
		Green	£440
		Blue	£750
		Cream	£190

158 Riley Saloon, green, excellent in tape repaired box. Sold for £80 Special Auction Services

30c Daimler, green, VG unboxed. Sold for £70 Special Auction Services

Ref.	First Issued	Model	TPG
24d	1934	**Vogue Saloon.** Unboxed	
		Blue	£90
		Violet	£480
		Blue, maroon chassis	£140
		Maroon	£110
		Brown	£70
		Yellow, brown chassis	£340
		Pink, green chassis	£220
		Cream	£500
		Green	£140
24e	1934	**Super Streamlined Saloon.** Unboxed	
		Maroon, green chassis	£130
		Yellow, red chassis	£190
		Red, maroon chassis	£100
		Maroon, black chassis	£560
		Green, maroon chassis	£460
		Red, black chassis	£850
24f	1934	**Sportsman Coupe,** various 2-tone colours. Unboxed	
		Red, black chassis	£240
		Blue, black chassis	£340
		Cream, black (repainted) chassis	£90
		Tan, blue chassis	£540
24g	1934	**4-Seater Sports Tourer,** various 2-tone colours. Unboxed	
		Blue, brown chassis	£560
		Cream, green chassis	£320
		Yellow, black chassis	£110
		Yellow, brown chassis	£110
		Cream, red chassis	£360
		Blue, black chassis	£130
24h	1934	**2-Seater Sports Tourer** 1st type casting. Unboxed	
		Green	£120
		Yellow, maroon chassis	£750
		Red, black chassis	£320
		Yellow, green chassis. Sold in 2003	£520
		Yellow, black chassis. Sold in 2003	£680
25j	1947	**Jeep,** red, green or lt blue versions. Yellow picture box	£75

www.toypriceguide.co.uk

30c Daimler, beige, black chassis, type 3 open chassis, smooth black hubs, minor paint touch-ins, unboxed. Sold for £240 DJ Auctions

Pre-war 24e Super Streamlined Saloon, green/black with criss-cross chassis, good condition with slight re-touching, no box. Sold for £180 Special Auction Services

25y	1952	**Universal Jeep,** red & green versions. Yellow picture box..£70
27f	1950	**Estate Car** (later renumbered 344), tan. Unboxed £40
		Supplied in trade boxes of 6. Sold complete in 2007 ....£180
		Rare 344/27f yellow dual numbered box with model £110
30a	1935	**Chrysler Airflow Saloon,** open chassis, cut-in grill. Unboxed.
		Pre-war 1st type smooth painted hubs - dk. brown, cream, lt. blue, green, maroon, turquoise
		& violet versions £110-130
		Pre-war 1st type smooth painted hubs - rare red version. Sold in 2008......................................£170
		Post war black ridged hubs - cream & green version £90-110
		Post war black ridged hubs - rare mid blue version. Sold in 2009 ....£480
30b	1935	**Rolls Royce,** black open chassis version. Unboxed. £70-90
		Sea Green £320
		Dk green...£170
		Mid blue..£160
		Lt blue..£260
30b	1946	**Rolls Royce,** silver hub versions, various colours. Unboxed £60-80
30c	1935	**Daimler,** smooth hubs, various 2-tone colours. Unboxed. £70-100
30d	1935	**Vauxhall,** spare wheel, various 2-tone colours. Unboxed. £70-100
32	1934	**Chrysler Airflow Saloon** (formerly 30a) dk red. Unboxed. £80-100
35a	1936	**Saloon Car,** with or without spare wheel cover, various colours. Unboxed £50-60
35az	1939	**2-Seater Fiat Saloon,** SIMCA cast inside, blue, green or red. Unboxed....................................£60-70
35b	1936	**Racer,** blue, red, silver or yellow. Unboxed £60
35b	1939	Midget Racer (later renumbered 200), silver. Unboxed. £50-60
		* Add £100 for scarce green version
35c	1936	**MG Sports Car,** red, blue, black, green & yellow, white rubber tyres. Unboxed. £30-40
35d	1938	**Austin 7 with wire windscreen frame,** various colours. Unboxed. £50-60
		* Reduce price guide by £15 for later models without wire windscreen
36a	1937	**Armstrong Siddeley Limousine** with tinplate driver & footman. Unboxed.
		Maroon £220
		Green, maroon chassis £580
		Maroon, black chassis £200
		Also issued for a short time after the war to use up left over parts, identifiable by smooth wheels and slots in the baseplate for driver and passengers

36a Armstrong Siddeley, mid blue, black chassis, black ridged hubs, excellent unboxed. Sold for £60 DJ Auctions

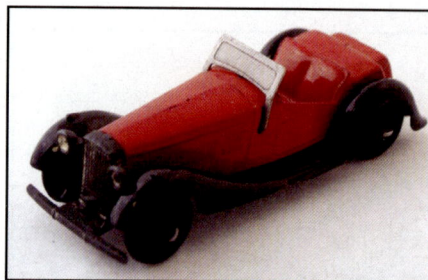

36e British Salmson 2-Seater, red, black chassis, black ridged hubs, excellent unboxed. Sold for £85 DJ Auctions

Ref.	First Issued	Model	TPG
36a	1947	**Armstrong Siddeley Limousine no figures,** grey & various 2-tone colours	£130-160
36b	1937	**2-seater Bentley Sport Coupe** with tinplate driver & footman. Unboxed	
		Cream, black chassis	£460
		Grey	£1,900
		Yellow, maroon chassis	£820
		Green, black chassis	£500
36b	1947	**Bentley without driver & footman,** various 2-tone colours	£130-160
36c	1937	**Humber Vogue Saloon with tinplate driver & footman.** Unboxed	
		Lilac, black (repainted) chassis	£660
		Violet	£270
		Green	£720
36c	1947	**Humber Vogue without driver & footman,** various 2-tone colours	£110-130
36d	1937	**Rover Streamlined Saloon with driver & footman.** Unboxed.	
		Green	£260
		Green, black chassis	£460
		Blue, black chassis	£240
		Red, black chassis	£330
36d	1946	**Rover without driver & footman,** various green & blue 2-tone versions.	£100-120
36e	1937	**2-Seater British Salmson Sports Car with driver.** Unboxed	
		Black, red chassis	£850
		Red, black chassis	£750
		Red, maroon chassis	£900
		Blue	£580
36e	1946	**British Salmson without driver,** various 2-tone colours.Unboxed	£100-130
		* Add £50 to price guide for scarce brown or red issues	
36f	1937	**4-Seater British Salmson Sports Car with driver.** Unboxed	
		Red	£200
		Green	£750
		Violet	£520
		Supplied in trade boxes of 6. Price for trade box containing 3 models. Sold in 2000	£820
36f	1947	**4-Seater British Salmson Sports Car without driver,** various colours. Unboxed	£70-90
38a	1937	**Frazer Nash BMW Sports,** various colours. Unboxed. Later 1946/7 versions have HORNBY SERIES on baseplate	£70-90

www.toypriceguide.co.uk

38a Frazer-Nash, blue, VG (few minor chips), unboxed. Sold for £75 Special Auction Services

38d Alvis Sports Tourer, leaf green, mid green hubs, VG unboxed. Sold for £70 Wallis & Wallis

38b	1940	**Sunbeam Talbot Sports** (renumbered 101) flat or ridged hubs, red, grey & green versions. Unboxed......£60-70
38c	1946	**Lagonda Sports Coupe** (renumbered 102) flat or ridged hubs, green & grey versions. U/b.......£65-85
38d	1946	**Alvis Sports Tourer,** dk green, maroon & red versions, black hubs. Unboxed. ....£50-70 In various colours with black wheel hubs, early 1950s export models were issued with coloured hub colours matching bodywork shades
38e	1946	**Armstrong Siddlely Coupe** (renumbered 104), grey, green, red, cream & blue versions.U/b.....£60-70
38f	1941	**Jaguar SS100 Sports Car** (later re-numbered 105), black flat hubs. Unboxed £70-90

Pale Grey, red interior version...£620
Pale Grey, black interior version..£70
Red...£170
Mid blue..£130
Dk blue..£190
Maroon..£60
Beige..£110
Khaki..£100

39a	1939	**Packard Super 8 Tourer,** black flat hubs, green, yellow, black, blue & grey versions. Unboxed £90-120 Dk green version..£280
39a	1947	**Packard Super 8 Tourer,** black ridged hubs, green & brown versions. Unboxed £50-70
39b	1939	**Oldsmobile 6 Sedan,** flat hubs, green, dk red, black, yellow, blue & grey versions. Unboxed £125-150
39b	1947	**Oldsmobile 6 Sedan,** black ridged hubs, green, dk red, black, cream, blue & grey versions. Unboxed..£70-90 Rare 2-tone blue version made for the US market £260
39c	1939	**Lincoln Zephyr Coupe,** black flat hubs. Unboxed

Maroon..£60
Grey...£50

| 39cu | | 2-tone red version made for the US market. Unboxed, sold in 2008 ....£2,000 |
| 39c | 1947 | **Lincoln Zephyr Coupe,** black ridged hubs, grey, red & brown versions. Yellow picture box.£60-80 |

2-tone maroon/cream...£60
2-tone green/cream..£60
2-tone blue..£60

| 39d | 1939 | **Buick Viceroy Saloon,** black flat hubs, red, cream, green, blue, grey versions. Unboxed. ..£80-120 *Expect to pay £300 for sand coloured version |
| 39d | 1947 | **Buick Viceroy Saloon,** black ridged hubs, red, tan, green, blue, grey versions. Unboxed.....£60-80 |

39e Chrysler Royal Sedan, blue, fatigued condition. Sold for £80 Special Auction Services

102 MG Midget, rare light green version, excellent unboxed. Sold for £225 Special Auction Services

Ref.	First Issued	Model	TPG

39e	1939	**Chrysler Royal Sedan,** unboxed.	£100-125
		Black, black hubs	£150
		Light blue, blue hubs	£170
		Cream, green hubs	£300
		Grey, black hubs	£100
		Green, black hubs	£60
		Violet blue, black hubs	£170
	1947	US issue: 2-tone green, green hubs	£110
		Dutch promotional issue in chrome for Hausmann & Hotte. Sold in 2008	£580
39f	-	**Studebaker State Commander.** Unboxed	
	1939	Black flat hub versions in grey, green & yellow	£140-180
	1946	Black ridged hub versions in grey, green, blue, red, brown & yellow	£60-90
40a	1947	**Riley Saloon** (later renumbered 158), green, blue & cream colour versions. Unboxed.	£60-90
40b	1948	**Triumph 1800 Saloon** (later renumbered 151), tan, blue, grey versions. Unboxed	£60-90
		* Add £100 to price guide for black version	
40d	1949	**Austin A40 Devon** (later re-numbered 152), grey, blue & green versions. Unboxed.	£40-50
		* Add £100 to price guide for maroon version	
		Supplied to retailers in trade boxes of 6. Price for a complete trade box	£150
40e	1948	**Standard Vanguard** (later re-numbered 153), tan & blue versions. Unboxed.	£50-80
		* Add £100 to price guide for cream, dk red & dk blue versions	
		Versions released in yellow colour spot box	£180
40f	1951	**Hillman Minx** (later re-numbered 154), green & brown versions. Unboxed	£100-120
		Supplied to retailers in trade boxes of 6. Price for a single model in a trade box	£140
40g	1950	**Morris Oxford** (later re-numbered 159), dk green, grey & brown versions. Unboxed.	£70-90
		* Add £100 to price guide for mid green version	
40j	1953	**Austin A40 Somerset** (later re-numbered 161), blue & red versions. Yellow picture box	£90-130
101	1957	**Sunbeam Alpine.** Yellow picture box. Maroon.	£95
		* Add £40 to price guide for spun hub version	
		Turquoise or lt blue	£120
		Mid blue	£120
102	1957	**MG Midget,** green & yellow versions. Unboxed	£120-150
		Pale green or yellow versions in rare colour spot box. Sold in 2008	£1,000

106 Austin Atlantic, black, red seats, red ridged hubs, mint in yellow box in correct colour spot. Sold for £170 DJ Auctions

108 MG Midget, white, RN28, excellent in a fair box. Sold for £120 Special Auction Services

103	1957	**Austin Healey 100.** Yellow picture box	
		Cream	£160
		Red	£140
104	1957	**Aston Martin DB3S.** Yellow picture box	
		Pink	£120
		Lt blue	£140
105	1957	**Triumph TR2.** Yellow picture box	
		Grey	£180
		Yellow	£220
106	1954	**Austin A90 Atlantic** (formerly 140a). Yellow picture box	
		Black	£130
		Lt blue	£120
		Pink	£160
107	1955	**Sunbeam Alpine Sports with race number 24 or 34.** Yellow picture box	
		Pink	£100
		Lt blue	£100
108	1955	**MG Midget,** driver with race number 24, 26 or 28. Yellow picture box.	
		Cream	£100
		Red	£180
		US issue: Cream, no driver or race no. Unboxed sold in 2009	£220
		US issue: Red, no driver or race no. Boxed sold in 2008	£400
109	1955	**Austin Healey 100 with race number 21, 22, 23 or 28.** Yellow picture box	
		Cream	£130
		Yellow	£100
110	1956	**Aston Martin DB3S with race number 20, 22 or 25.** Yellow picture box	
		Grey, blue interior	£110
		Mid Green, red interior	£100
		Pale green, blue interior (scare colour variation)	£220
110	1966	**Aston Martin DB5,** wire wheels. Plastic case & window box versions	
		Metallic red	£65
		Blue	£65
		Metallic red in window box with rare 'Mr Dealer' card still attached. Sold in 2004	£170
111	1956	**Triumph TR2 Sports Car with race number 25 or 29.** Yellow picture box	
		Blue	£190
		Pink	£240

113 MGB, cream with red interior, excellent in a good box. Sold for £75 Special Auction Services

114 Triumph Spitfire, silver, excellent in a good box. Sold for £80 Special Auction Services

Ref.	First Issued	Model	TPG
112	1961	**Austin Healey Sprite Mk2,** red. Yellow picture & window box versions	£100
		SA issue: Turquoise, yellow picture box. Sold in 2008	£1,800
		SA issue: Lilac, yellow picture box. Sold in 2003	£750
		SA issue: Dk blue, yellow picture box. Sold in 2003	£1,200
113	1962	**MGB Sports Car.** Yellow / red picture box	
		Yellow	£400
		White or cream	£70
		Promotional issue: chrome plated (unboxed)	£140
		SA issue: Red, cream interior. Sold in 2008	£1,300
		5' 9d Shop display leaflet showing model	£25
114	1963	**Triumph Spitfire,** plastic driver. Window & yellow / red picture box versions	
		Gold / bronze, with or without 'Tiger in Your Tank' boot logo	£80
		Red	£70
		Metallic grey	£60
		Metallic lilac	£160
115	1965	**Plymouth Fury Sports,** driver & passenger figures, white. Yellow picture box	£70
116	1966	**Volvo P1800S,** wire wheels, red & metallic red versions. Plastic case	£55
120	1962	**Jaguar E Type with detachable hardtop.** Yellow / red & yellow picture box versions.	
		Red / black or red / grey roof versions	£100
		Metallic blue version in early type window box. Sold in 2004	£660
122	1977	**Volvo 265DL Estate,** metallic blue & orange versions. Window / header card box	£20
123	1977	**Princess 2200HL,** bronze & white versions. Window / header card box	£30
		White pre-production model with POLICE decal on doors sold in 2009	£100
124	1977	**Rolls Royce Phantom V,** metallic blue. Window / header card box	£25
127	1964	**Rolls Royce Silver Cloud MK3.** Plastic case & double ended window box versions	
		Gold	£45
		Red	£45
		Turquoise	£80
128	1964	**Mercedes Benz 600,** 3 figures & luggage. Plastic case & window box & bubble pack versions. * Later issues with Speedwheels	
		Metallic red	£45
		Metallic blue	£30
129	1965	**Volkswagen 1300 Sedan,** metallic blue. Plastic case. * Later issues with Speedwheels	£35

133 Cunningham C-3R, white, blue stripes, tan seats, driver, blue hubs, mint in a dirty box.
Sold for £70 DJ Auctions

131 Jaguar E-Type, white, red interior, mint in mint perspex box with laurel label.
Sold for £65 Special Auction Services

130	1964	**Ford Consul Corsair.** Yellow/red picture box	
		Metallic red	£100
		Blue	£45
131	1956	**Cadillac Eldorado,** driver, coloured hubs, yellow & pink versions. Yellow box.	£90
131	1968	**Jaguar E Type 2+2,** wire wheels. Plastic case & bubble pack version.	
		* Later issues with Speedwheels	
		White	£60
		Metallic purple	£70
		Gold/bronze	£120
132	1955	**Packard Convertible,** green & brown versions. Yellow box	£90
132	1967	**Ford 40RV,** silver pink & blue versions. Plastic case	£45
133	1955	**Cunningham C5R,** white, blue hubs, bonnet stripes, race no. 31. Yellow box	£55
133	1964	**Ford Cortina** (replaced 139), gold & lt green versions. Colour picture box	£85
134	1964	**Triumph Vitesse,** lt blue. Yellow/red picture box	£70-80
		Green with white flash version in colour picture box. Pre Nicky Toys test model made in India.	£420
135	1963	**Triumph 2000 Saloon.** Yellow/red picture box.	
		Metallic turquoise/white roof	£50
		Metallic green/white roof	£50
		Promotional issue: cherry red, white roof	£1,000
		Promotional issue: black, white roof	£800
		Promotional issue: black, green roof	£480
		Promotional issue: white, black roof	£600
		Promotional issue: white, grey roof	£750
		Promotional issue: chrome plated	£1500-2000
		Promotional issue: light blue, black roof	£360
136	1964	**Vauxhall Viva,** metallic blue & white/grey versions. Yellow or colour picture box versions	£55
137	1963	**Plymouth Fury Convertible,** grey, blue, pink & green versions. Yellow picture box	£70
138	1963	**Hillman Imp,** plastic luggage, metallic silver, blue & red versions. Colour picture, yellow, yellow/red & window box versions.	£70-100
		Metallic red	£60
		Metallic green	£50
		Metallic silver	£60
		Metallic blue	£150
		For standard range models in double ended yellow/red 'Export' window boxes	£90-110

138 Hillman Imp with suitcase in bonnet, metallic green, excellent in a good box. Sold for £55 Special Auction Services

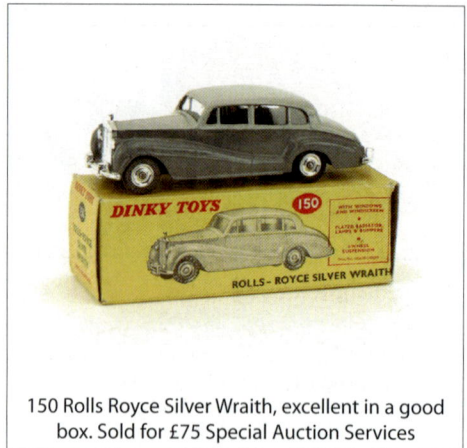

150 Rolls Royce Silver Wraith, excellent in a good box. Sold for £75 Special Auction Services

Ref.	First Issued	Model	TPG

139   1963   **Ford Consul Cortina,** metallic & non metallic blue versions. Yellow picture box £70

139a   1949   **Ford Fordor Sedan** (later renumbered 170), large & small baseplate lettering, various colours all with matching hubs. Unboxed.
Mid Green £30
Pale green.. £60
Red £120
2-tone red / cream 'Highline' version £100
Tan.. £160
Yellow £100
Trade box of 6 models. Sold in 2006 .... £380

139b   1950   **Hudson Commodore,** blue, cream & grey versions with coloured roof. Unboxed £50
Supplied to retailers in trade boxes of 6. Price for a complete trade box £440

140   1963   **Morris 1100, blue.** Yellow picture box £65

140a   1951   **Austin A90 Atlantic** (renumbered 106), lt blue, red, pink & black versions. Unboxed.
Black £60
Light blue... £60
Pink £70
Red £150
Mid blue version, unboxed. Sold in 2009 .... £460
Supplied to retailers in trade boxes of 6. Complete trade box sold in 2009 .... £420
Mid blue version, unboxed. Sold in 2009 .... £460
* Add £100 for models in rare 106/140a dual numbered boxes.

140b   1951   **Rover 75 Saloon,** cream & maroon versions. Unboxed. £50-60
Supplied to retailers in trade boxes of 6. Price for a single model in a trade box £110
Cream version with red hubs. Sold in 2008 .... £1,100
Cream version with blue hubs. Sold in 2008 .... £100

141   1963   **Vauxhall Victor Estate,** yellow. Yellow / red picture box £60
Dk red LIGHTNING FASTERNERS promotional. Unboxed sold in 2004................................... £640

142   1962   **Jaguar Mk10.** Yellow / red & window box versions £60
Silver.. £120
Metallic blue £100
Lt metallic blue... £70
Sky blue South African issue. Sold in 2008 .... £700
For standard range models in double ended gold 'Export' window boxes £120

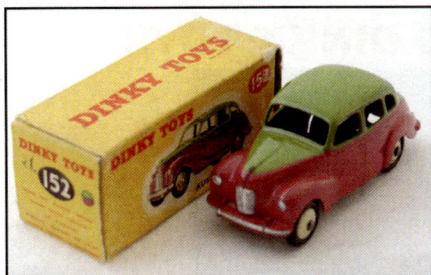

152 Austin Devon Saloon, 2-tone lime green & cerise, cream ridged hubs, mint in repaired yellow box with correct colour spot.
Sold for £200 DJ Auctions

152 Austin Devon Saloon, blue, excellent in a box missing end flap.
Sold for £55 Special Auction Services

143	1962	**Ford Capri,** lt blue/white roof version. Red/yellow & yellow picture box versions £60
144	1963	**Volkswagen 1500,** gold, white & bronze versions. Yellow/red picture box £60
145	1962	**Singer Vogue,** lt green. Yellow picture box £70
146	1963	**Daimler 2.5L V8,** metallic green. Yellow picture box £95
147	1962	**Cadillac '62,** metallic green. Yellow picture box £50-60

148	1962	**Ford Fairline.** Yellow picture box
		Pale green £60
		Metallic green £280
		Pale metallic green £100
		Grey South African issue. £460
		Dk blue South African issue £320
		For standard range models in double ended yellow/red 'Export' window boxes £80

149	1971	**Citroen Dyane,** bronze & grey versions, with or without Speedwheels. Colour picture box £25
150	1959	**Rolls Royce Silver Wraith,** 2-tone grey, metal & plastic bumper versions. Yellow picture box. £60

151	1954	**Triumph 1800 Saloon** (formerly 40b). Yellow picture box
		Blue £70
		Mid blue £130
		Tan £70
		Beige (unboxed) £35
		Grey (unboxed) £70
		Prussian Blue (unboxed) £240

151	1965	**Vauxhall Victor 101,** yellow & red versions. Yellow picture box £75

152	1954	**Austin A40 Devon** (formerly 40d).
		2-tone yellow/blue. Unboxed £45
		Green. Unboxed £50
		Beige. Unboxed £380
		Lt grey. Unboxed £45
		Pink/green. Yellow picture box £340
		Mid blue. Yellow picture box £580
		Dk blue. Yellow picture box £70
		Greyish green. Yellow picture box £240

152	1965	**Rolls Royce Phantom V,** driver, 2 passenger, dk blue. Plastic case £35
153	1954	**Standard Vanguard** (formerly 40e), tan, red, cream & blue versions. Yellow picture box £80
153	1967	**Aston Martin DB6,** spoked wheels, metallic silver & turquoise versions. Plastic case £65

TOY COLLECTORS FAIRS ARE A GREAT PLACE TO FIND DINKY TOYS

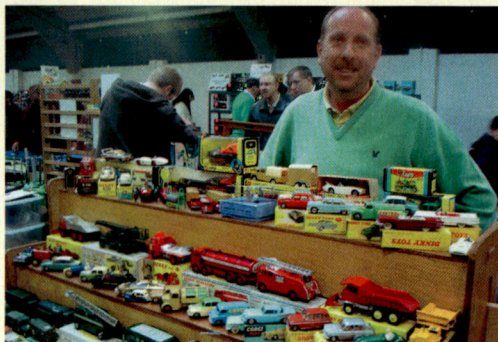

Barry Potter Fairs Toy Collectors Fairs for 2011

January

Sunday	2nd	Buxton
Tuesday	4th	Rugby evening
Sunday	9th	Kettering
Sunday	16th	Stafford Showground
Sunday	23rd	Coventry

February

Sunday	6th	Harrogate
Sunday	13th	NEC Birmingham
Saturday	19th	Sandown Park
Sunday	20th	Reebok Stadium, Bolton
Sunday	27th	Buxton

March

Tuesday	1st	Rugby evening
Sunday	13th	Stafford Showground
Sunday	27th	Leeds, Elland Road

April

Sunday	10th	Trafford Centre
Sunday	17th	Buxton
Sunday	24th	Harrogate

May

Tuesday	3rd	Rugby evening
Sunday	8th	Coventry
Sunday	15th	Rugby Vintage
Saturday	21st	Sandown Park

June

Sunday	5th	NEC Birmingham
Sunday	12th	Stafford Showground
Sunday	19th	Buxton

July

Sunday	3rd	Reebok Stadium, Bolton
Tuesday	5th	Rugby evening
Sunday	10th	Coventry
Sunday	17th	Leeds, Elland Road

August

Sunday	14th	Stafford Showground

September

Saturday	3rd	Sandown Park
Sunday	4th	Trafford Centre
Sunday	11th	Buxton
Tuesday	13th	Rugby evening
Sunday	18th	Coventry
Sunday	25th	NEC Birmingham

October

Saturday	1st	Rugby Vintage
Sunday	2nd	Stafford Showground
Sunday	16th	Reebok Stadium
Sunday	30th	Leeds, Elland Road

November

Tuesday	1st	Rugby evening
Sunday	13th	Buxton
Saturday	19th	Sandown Park
Sunday	20th	Kettering
Sunday	27th	Harrogate

December

Sunday	4th	Trafford Centre
Sunday	11th	Stafford Showground
Tuesday	27th	NEC Birmingham
Thursday	29th	Reebok Stadium

Barry Potter Fairs www.bpfairs.com Tel: 01604 846688

154 Hillman Minx Saloon, 2-tone cerise & pale blue, blue ridged hubs, mint in excellent yellow box with correct colour spot. Sold for £280 DJ Auctions

159 Morris Oxford Saloon, 2-tone green & cream, green ridged hubs, mint in excellent yellow box with correct colour spot. Sold for £190 DJ Auctions

Ref.	First Issued	Model	TPG
154	1955	**Hillman Minx** (formerly 40f) Yellow picture box.	
		2-tone blue/pink. Unboxed	£170
		Tan	£120
		2-tone green/cream	£160
		Mid green	£190
154	1966	**Ford Taunus,** yellow with white roof. Yellow picture box	£50
155	1961	**Ford Anglia 105E.** Yellow picture box	£65-75
		Green	£150
		Grey (South African issue)	£170
156	1954	**Rover 75** (formerly 140b), Yellow picture box	£70-90
		Cream	£260
		2-tone green, green hubs	£100
		2-tone cream/blue	£100
		Maroon	£300
		2-tone cream/violet. Sold in 2006	£620
		2-tone green/cream. Sold in 2006	£220
156	1968	**Saab 96,** metallic red & blue versions. Plastic case	£60
157	1954	**Jaguar XK120,** Yellow/red & yellow picture box versions	£90-110
		Red	£100
		Yellow	£70
		Green	£190
		2-tone lt blue/pink	£150
		2-tone yellow/grey	£120
		White	£140
157	1968	**BMW 2000 Tilux.** Colour picture box with inner diorama tray	
		Blue/white	£55
		All blue version	£85
158	1954	**Riley Saloon** (formerly 40a), cream, blue, grey & green versions. Yellow picture box	£95
158	1967	**Rolls Royce Silver shadow,** metallic red & blue versions. Plastic case	£55
		Pre-production model in gold	£190
159	1954	**Morris Oxford** (formerly 40g), green & brown versions. Yellow box	£90-110
		2-tone issues	£140-160
		Blue	£780
160	1958	**Austin A30,** tan & turquoise versions. Yellow picture box	£80-100

168 Singer Gazelle, 2-tone, grey & green, spun hubs, mint in tape repaired yellow box.
Sold for £90 DJ Auctions

161 Austin Somerset, black/cream, excellent unboxed. Sold for £95 Special Auction Services

Ref.	First Issued	Model	TPG
160	1967	**Mercedes Benz 250SE,** metallic blue. Plastic case & bubble pack versions £40-60	
161	1954	**Austin A40 Somerset** (formerly 40j), blue & red versions. Yellow picture box £75	
		2-tone red/yellow £240	
		2-tone black/white £200	
161	1965	**Ford Mustang Fastback,** white & yellow versions. Window box & Plastic case versions.	
		* Reduce price guide by £20 for later orange Speedwheels version £50	
162	1956	**Ford Zephyr Mk1,** cream or blue 2-tone versions. Yellow picture box...........................£80	
162	1966	**Triumph 1300,** lt blue. Yellow picture box...........................£80	
163	1956	**Bristol 450 Coupe,** racing number 27, green. Yellow picture box...........................£130	
163	1966	**Volkswagen 1600TL,** red, metallic red & blue versions. Yellow picture box...........................£50	
164	1957	**Vauxhall Cresta,** red/cream & green/grey 2-tone versions. Yellow picture box...........................£90-110	
164	1966	**Ford Zodiac Mk4,** metallic blue, bronze & silver versions. Plastic case...........................£50-60	
165	1959	**Humber Hawk,** black/green & red/cream 2-tone versions. Yellow picture box...........................£90-110	
165	1969	**Ford Capri,** metallic purple, blue & green versions. Colour picture box...........................£80	
166	1958	**Sunbeam Rapier,** blue & yellow versions. Yellow picture box...........................£90	
166	1967	**Renault R16,** metallic blue. Colour picture box...........................£45	
167	1958	**AC Aceca Sports Coupe,** cream/maroon & grey/red versions.	
		Yellow picture colour spot box...........................£90	
		Yellow picture box with uncoloured spot...........................£170	
		Red/yellow box...........................£130	
168	1959	**Singer Gazelle Saloon,** green & brown versions. Yellow picture box...........................£75	
168	1968	**Ford Escort,** white, lt blue & metallic red versions. Bubble pack. £50	
		* Reduce price guide by £20 for later Speedwheels version	
169	1958	**Studebaker Golden Hawk,** green & tan versions. Yellow picture box...........................£75	
169	1967	**Ford Corsair 2000E,** silver. Colour picture box...........................£60	
170	1954	**Ford Fordor Saloon,** red (formerly 139a), yellow, green & tan versions. Yellow picture box. £75	
		* Add £50 to price guide for 2-tone versions	
170	1964	**Lincoln Continental,** bronze & lt blue versions. Window & perspex box versions...........................£55	

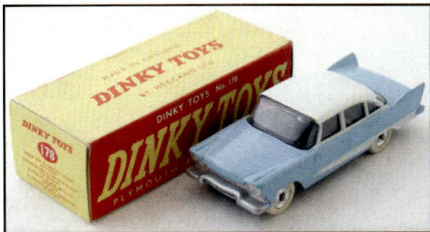

Scarce 178 Plymouth Plaza, light blue, white roof & flash, spun hubs, white tyres, mint in excellent red/yellow box. Sold for £290 DJ Auctions

180 Packard Clipper Sedan, 2-tone cream & cerise, VG in a worn box. Sold for £70 Wallis & Wallis

171	1954	**Hudson Commodore Sedan** (formerly 139b), navy/tan & cream/brown 2-tone versions. Yellow picture box.	£55
171	1965	**Austin 1800,** metallic blue versions. Colour picture box	£60
172	1954	**Studebaker Land Cruise,** blue & green versions. Yellow picture box.	£60
		* For 2-tone versions add £50 to price guide	
172	1965	**Fiat 2300 Station Wagon,** 2-tone blue. Double ended window & picture box versions	£80
173	1958	**Nash Rambler Station Wagon,** pink & lt blue versions. Yellow picture box.	£50
		* Add £100 to price guide for beige version	
173	1969	**Pontiac Parisienne,** metallic red & blue versions. Colour picture box	£50
174	1958	**Hudson Hornet,** cream hubs, red or yellow 2-tone versions. Yellow picture box.	£55
174	1969	**Ford Mercury Cougar,** blue, Speedwheels, retractable aerial. Colour picture box	£50
175	1958	**Hillman Minx,** coloured hubs, grey or brown 2-tone versions. Yellow picture box.	£70
175	1969	**Cadillac Eldorado,** metallic green & purple versions, Speedwheels. Colour picture box	£45
176	1958	**Austin A105 Saloon,** cream or grey 2-tone versions. Yellow picture box	£80
		The first Dinky Toy to have fully glazed windows	
176	1969	**NSU Ro80,** metallic red. Colour picture box.	£45
177	1961	**Opel Kapitan,** grey. Yellow picture box	£45
178	1959	**Plymouth Plaza,** pink, blue & tan 2-tone versions. Yellow picture box.	£100
178	1975	**Mini Clubman,** Speedwheels, bronze. Window box & bubble pack versions.	£35
		* Add £20 to price guide for red version	
		Pale grey pre-production model sold in 2008	£80
		Pale blue pre-production model sold in 2008	£90
		20x15cm poster showing this model produced for retail display	£30
179	1958	**Studebaker President,** coloured hubs, yellow & blue versions. Yellow picture box.	£65
179	1971	**Opel Commodore,** Speedwheels, metallic blue. Colour picture box	£55
180	1958	**Packard Clipper,** coloured hubs, orange or pink 2-tone versions. Yellow picture box.	£100
180	1979	**Rover 3500,** white. Window box.	£30
181	1956	**Volkswagen Saloon,** coloured hubs, blue, green & grey versions. Yellow picture box.	£60
182	1958	**Porsche 356a Coupe,** plain & coloured hubs, pink, blue, red, cream. Yellow picture box/colour spot versions.	£80
		* Add £50 to price guide for metal hub versions	

175 Cadillac Eldorado, metallic purple,
excellent in a chipped perspex box.
Sold for £55 Special Auction Services

187 De Tomaso Mangusta, pink/white,
excellent in VG perspex box.
Sold for £35 Special Auction Services

Ref.	First Issued	Model	TPG
183	1958	**Fiat 600,** red & green versions. Yellow picture box	£60
183	1966	**Morris Minor** (Automatic), blue & red versions. Yellow picture box	£75
184	1961	**Volvo 122,** red. Yellow picture box.	£100
		SA issue: mid blue, unboxed	£160
185	1961	**Alfa Romeo 1900 Sprint,** yellow & red versions. Yellow picture box	£75
186	1961	**Mercedes Benz 220SE,** various blue versions. Yellow picture box	£60
187	1959	**VW Karmann Ghia Coupe,** green & red versions. Yellow picture box	£70
187	1968	**De Tomaso Mangusta 5000,** pink. Plastic case	£35
188	1968	**Jensen FF,** Speedwheels, yellow. Plastic case	£60
189	1959	**Triumph Herald Saloon,** green & blue versions. Yellow picture box.	£70-80

Hornby enjoyed a close working relationship with Standard Triumph resulting in the range of Dinky models being on sale in toy shops at the same time as the 'real thing' hit car show rooms. Dinky supplied Standard Triumph with a limited number of models in the full range of Herald colours, many of which were given away to early car purchasers. As a result these special colour versions are highly sought after by collectors with prices as follows:

		Grey/blue upper body, lt grey mid body, chrome hubs. Yellow picture box	£850
		Dk blue roof & side panels with white bonnet & boot, chrome hubs. Red/yellow box	£1,500
		Lilac upper body & pale grey bonnet & boot, chrome hubs. Yellow picture box	£380
		Grey/green upper body & pale grey bonnet & boot, chrome hubs. Yellow/red box	£700
		Purple upper body & ivory bonnet & boot, chrome hubs. Yellow picture box	£850
		Fern green upper body & white bonnet & boot, chrome hubs. Yellow picture box	£320
189	1969	**Lamborgini Marzal,** red/white, yellow/white & green/white versions, later issues with Speedwheels. Plastic case	£35
190	1970	**Monteverdi 375L,** metallic dk red, later issues with Speedwheels. Plastic case	£35
191	1959	**Dodge Royal Sedan,** green or cream versions with colour flash. Yellow picture box	£70
192	1959	**De Soto Fireflite,** lt blue & grey versions. Yellow picture box	£65
192	1970	**Range Rover,** Speedwheels, black, bronze & yellow versions. With or without rooflight.	
		Colour picture box versions	£40
		Window box versions	£20

189 Triumph Herald, light blue/white, good
in VG red/yellow box.
Sold for £65 Special Auction Services

191 Dodge Royal Sedan, cream, tan flash, spun
hubs, white tyres, mint in excellent yellow box.
Sold for £100 DJ Auctions

193	1961	**Rambler Station Wagon,** yellow. Yellow picture box £60
194	1961	**Bentley S Coupe,** seated driver, bronze. Yellow picture box...£90
195	1961	**Jaguar 3.4 Mk2,** grey, dk red & cream versions. Yellow picture box £80
196	1963	**Holden Special Sedan,** turquoise & gold versions with white roof. Yellow picture box £80
197	1961	**Morris Mini Traveller,** cream with red interior. Yellow picture box ....
		Fluorescent green..£150
		Cream £70
		Dk green..£240
198	1962	**Rolls Royce Phantom V,** 2-tone metallic cream or grey versions. Yellow picture box £75
		The first Dinky Toy produced in metallic paint
199	1961	**Austin 7 Countryman,** blue or blue/grey version. Yellow picture box.......................................£50
		Red £190
		Pink £130
		Orange model in 'Colour of Model may Differ from Illustration' stickered box........................£260
200	1954	**Midget Racer** (formerly 35b), silver. Unboxed £30
		Supplied to retailers in trade boxes of 6. Price for a complete trade box £130
200	1971	**Matra 630 Le Mans,** Speedwheels, blue. Colour picture box & plastic case versions £40
201	1979	**Plymouth Stock Car,** race number 34, blue. Window box £20
202	1971	**Fiat Arbarth 2000,** Speedwheels, red/white. Colour picture box...£35
202	1979	**Customised Land Rover,** yellow. Window box £20
203	1979	**Customised Range Rover,** black. Window box...£25
204	1971	**Ferrari 312P,** Speedwheels, metallic red, red or white door versions. Colour picture box..........£40
205	1962	**Talbot Lago Racing Car** (formerly 23k later renumbered 230), baseplate numbered 230, race
		number 4, blue. Blister card £190-230
		Rare mid blue version with red plastic hubs on blister card £700
205	1968	**Lotus Cortina Rally,** race number 7, Monte Carlo decal, white. Colour picture box £85
206	1962	**Maserati Racing Car** (formerly 23n later renumbered 231), baseplate numbered 231, red/white.
		Blister card £250-300
206	1978	**Customised Corvette,** red/yellow & white/black versions. Window box.....................................£20
207	1962	**Alfa Romeo Racing Car** (formerly 23f later renumbered 232), baseplate numbered 232, red.
		Blister card. £250-300

215 Ford GT, metallic green, RN7, mint boxed.
Sold for £55 Special Auction Services

231 Maserati Racing Car, red, white flash, RN9,
red ridged hubs, mint in excellent yellow box.
Sold for £170 DJ Auctions

Ref.	First Issued	Model	TPG
207	1977	**Triumph TR7 Rally,** race number 8, red/white/blue. Window box	£25
208	1962	**Cooper Bristol Racing Car** (formerly 23g later renumbered 233), baseplate numbered 233, green. Blister card	£250-300
208	1971	**VW Porsche 914,** with & without Speedwheels, yellow & blue versions. Window box & plastic case versions.	£30
209	1962	**Ferrari Racing Car** (formerly 23h later renumbered 234), baseplate numbered 234, race number 5, blue. Blister card	£250-300
210	1962	**Vanwall Racing Car** (renumbered 239), baseplate numbered 239, race number 5, green. Blister card	£190-230
210	1971	**Alfa Romeo 33 Tipo,** race number 36, red. Colour picture box	£40
211	1975	**Triumph TR7 Sports Car,** red. Window box. * Add £40 to price guide for blue & yellow versions Pre-production model, black with SAUDIA decals in standard issue window box	£35 £80
212	1965	**Ford Cortina Rally,** race number 8, white, East African Safari Rally decal. Colour picture box	£70
213	1970	**Ford Capri Rally,** race no.20, red & bronze, later models with Speedwheels. Plastic case	£45
214	1966	**Hillman Imp Rally,** race no.35, blue, Monte Carlo Rally decal. Colour picture box	£80
215	1965	**Ford GT Racing Car,** race no.7, green, white, blue & yellow versions. Plastic case	£35
216	1967	**Ferrari Dino,** spoked or Speedwheels, red & blue/black versions. Plastic case	£35
217	1968	**Alfa Romeo Scarabeo OSI,** spoked or Speedwheels, pink. Plastic case	£30
218	1969	**Lotus Europa,** Speedwheels, yellow & blue versions. Colour picture box	£30
219	1977	**Leyland Jaguar XJ 5.3,** white. Window box	£35
219	1980	**Jaguar Car,** white with red/black big cat logo on bonnet. Shrink wrapped on card This model was issued in 1980 after the Meccano Company had gone into receivership	£50
220	1954	**Small Open Racing Car** (formerly 23a), race no 4, silver & red versions. Yellow picture box	£45
220	1970	**Ferrari P5,** plain or Speedwheels, red. Plastic case.	£35
221	1954	**Speed of the Wind Racing Car** (formerly 23e), silver. Unboxed	£35
221	1969	**Corvette Stingray,** spoked or Speedwheels, red, white & gold versions. Plastic case	£35

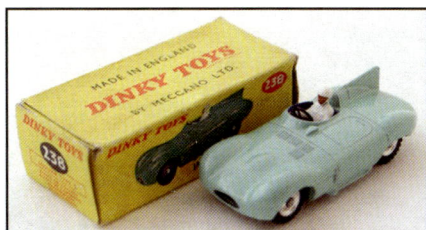

238 Jaguar D Type, turquoise, spun hubs, mint in crushed yellow box. Sold for £200 DJ Auctions

240 Cooper Racing Car, blue, RN 20, mint boxed. Sold for £45 Special Auction Services

222	1954	**Streamlined Racing Car** (formerly 22s), silver. Unboxed £35-45
		Supplied to retailers in trade boxes of 6. Price for a complete trade box £220
222	1978	**Hesketh 308E,** race number 2, bronze or blue. Window box. £20
		OLYMPUS CAMERAS version..£40
223	1970	**McClaren M8A Can-Am,** green & white, later models with Speedwheels. Plastic case.............£30
224	1970	**Mercedes Benz C111,** red & white versions. Plastic case £35
225	1971	**Lotus F1 Racing Car,** race no.7, green, red & blue versions. Colour picture box £35
226	1972	**Ferrari 312B2,** race number 5, red, gold & bronze versions. Colour picture box.........................£35
		Pre-production model in black plastic with race no. 2 decal sold in 2008 ....£125
227	1975	**Beach Buggy,** various 2-tone colour versions. Window box..£15
228	1970	**Super Sprinter,** Speedwheels, 2-tone blue versions. Plastic case...£30
230	1954	**Talbot Lago Racing Car** (formerly 23k & later 205), race no.4, blue. Yellow picture box. £85
231	1954	**Maserati Racing Car** (formerly 23n & later 206), race no.9, red/white. Yellow picture box. £90
232	1954	**Alfa Romeo Racing Car** (formerly 23f & later 207), race no.8, red. Yellow picture box. £85
233	1954	**Cooper Bristol Racing Car** (formerly 23g & later 208), race no.6, green. Yellow picture box. ...£80
234	1954	**Ferrari Racing Car** (formerly 23h & later 209), race no.5, blue. Yellow picture box. £90
		* Add £150 to price guide for models with yellow or white triangle on nose
235	1954	**HWM Racing Car** (formerly 23j), race no.7, green. Yellow picture box.....................................£75
236	1956	**Connaught Racing Car,** driver, race.32, green. Yellow picture box £70
237	1957	**Mercedes Benz Racing Car,** race no.30, white. Yellow picture box...£70
238	1957	**Jaguar D Type,** driver, race no.4, turquoise. Yellow picture box £90
239	1958	**Vanwall Racing Car** (formerly 210), race no.25, 26 or 35, green. Yellow picture box. £75
240	1963	**Cooper Racing Car,** race no.20, blue. Yellow/red picture box £70
241	1963	**Lotus Racing Car,** race no.7, 24, or 36, green. Yellow/red picture box £50
242	1963	**Ferrari Racing Car,** race no.36, red. Yellow/red picture box £60
243	1963	**BRM Racing Car,** race no.7, green. Yellow/red picture box...£45
281	1968	**PATHE NEWS Fiat Camera Car, black,** cameraman & camera. Picture box.............................£100
340	1954	**Land Rover** (formerly 27d), green & orange versions. Yellow picture box. £80
		Red version...£150

23E Trade box containg 6 mint 'Speed of ther Wind' Racing Cars in a good box with replacement inserts. Sold for £140 Toy Price Guide Archive

Dinky Gift Set 149 Sports Cars all in VG condition though the Triumph is missing tyres, box only fair. Sold for £340 Special Auction Services

Ref.	First Issued	Model	TPG
341	1954	**Land Rover Trailer** (formerly 27m), orange. Yellow picture box.	£25
		* Add £20 to price guide for red or dk green versions	
342	1966	**Austin Mini Moke,** green. Colour picture box or bubble packed	£40
344	1954	**Estate Car** (lformerly 27f), brown. Yellow picture box.	£55
370	1969	**Dragster Set complete with starter unit,** yellow / red. Colour picture box	£40
405	1954	**Universal Jeep** (formerly 25y), green & red versions. Yellow picture box	£90
475	1964	**Model T Ford,** 2 seated figures, blue. Window box	£35
476	1967	**Morris Oxford,** driver figure, yellow. Window box	£35
485	1964	**Santa's Model T Ford,** seated Santa, tree & presents load, red / white. Window box on card tray	£55

GIFT SETS

2	1946	**Private Automobiles Set;** 39a Packard, 39b Oldsmobile, 39c Lincoln, 39d Buick, 39e Chrysler. Green marble effect box	£3,400
		US Export version in blue box	£1,500
3	1947	**Private Automobiles set;** 30d Vauxhall, 36a Armstrong, 36b Bentley, 38a Frazer Nash, 39b Oldsmobile. Green / blue / orange marble effect box	£3,400
		US Export version in blue box	£2,600
3	1952	**Passenger Cars Set;** 27f Estate, 30h Ambulance, 40e Vanguard, 40g Morris Oxford, 40h Austin Taxi & 140b Rover. Blue / white stripe box with blue inner tray	£1,500
3	1952	**Passenger Cars Set;** 30d Vauxhall, 36b Bentley, 36d Rover, 38a Frazier Nash, 38c Lagonda. Blue marble effect box with green inner tray	£1250-1500
4	1953	**Racing Cars Set;** 23f Alfa, 23g Cooper Bristol, 23h Ferrari, 23j HWM & 23n Maserati. Blue / white stripe box with insert card	£850
22	1933	**Motor Vehicles Set;** 22a & 22b Sports Cars, 22c Truck, 22d Van, 22e Tractor & 22f Tank. Blue 'Modelled Miniatures' box	£9,000
23	1936	**Racing Cars Set;** 23c Mercedes, 23d auto Union & 23e Speed of Wind. Blue printed box	£510
24	1934	**Motor Cars Set;** 24a Ambulance, 24b Limousine, 24c Sedan, 24d Vogue, 24e Streamlined Saloon, 24f Coupe, 24g & 24h Tourers. Blue / gold marble effect picture label lid	£5,600
30	1935	**Motor Vehicle Set;** 30a Chrysler, 30b Rolls Royce, 30c Daimler, 30d Vauxhall, 30e Breakdown Truck & 30f Ambulance. Marble effect picture label lid	£2000-2250

Pre-war empty 24 Motor Cars set box, marbled purple/gold in fair condition. Sold for £650 Special Auction Services

No.47 Road signs (12) with filled in triangles, VG. Sold for £45 Special Auction Services

35	1935	**Small Cars Set;** 35a Saloon Car, 35b Racer & 35c MG. Green window box £440
121	1963	**Goodwood Racing Set;** 112 Austin Healy, 113 MGB, 120 Jaguar & 182 Porsche plus plastic figures. White card display box...£1,000
122	1963	**Touring Set;** 188 Caravan, 193 Station Wagon, 195 Jaguar, 270 AA Van, 295 Atlas & 796 Boat. Card display box with inner display £800
123	1963	**Mayfair Set;** 142 Jaguar, 150 & 198 Rolls Royce, 186 Mercedes, 194 Bentley & 199 Mini. Card display box with inner display...£750
124	1964	**Holiday Gift Set;** 952 Coach, 137 Plymouth, 142 Jaguar & 796 Boat. Illustrated plain card box with inner display stand..£560
125	1964	**Fun Ahoy Set;** 130 Ford Corsair & 796 Boat. Shrink wrapped open picture box £200
126	1971	**Motor Show Presentation Set;** 127 Rolls Royce, 151 Vauxhall Victor, 159 Cortina & 171 Austin 1800 in window box with inner diorama tray...£400
149	1958	**Sports Car Set;** 107 Sunbeam, 108 MG, 109 Austin Healey, 110 Aston Martin & 111 Triumph. Blue/white striped box...£1,100
188	1967	**Towaway Glider Set;**135 Triumph & trailer containing glider body & wings. Picture box with inner diorama tray...£160
201	1965	**Racing Cars;** 240 Cooper, 241 Lotus, 242 Ferrari & 243 BRM. Yellow window box with inner card tray diorama £380
237	1978	**Dinky Way Set;** 211 Triumph, 255 Police Mini, 382 Dump Truck & 412 AA Van, roadway, signs & decals. Shrink wrapped illustrated box...£75
245	1969	**Superfast Gift Set;** 131 Jauguar, 153 Aston Martin & 188 Jensen. Illustrated window box.......£140
246	1969	**International Gift Set;** 187 De Tomaso Mangusta, 215 Ford GT & 216 Ferrari Dino. Illustrated window box..£80
249	1955	**Racing Cars Set;** 231 Maserati, 232 Alfa, 233 Cooper Bristol, 234 Ferrari & 235 HWM. Blue/white striped box £750
-	-	**Mini Dinky, 12 car case containing;** 10 Corsair, 11 Jaguar, 12 Corvette, 13 Ferrari, 14 Chevrolet, 16 Mustang, 18 Mercedes, 19 MGB, 20 Cadillac, 21 Fiat, 22 Oldsmobile & 61 Lotus. Illustrated outer box containing models in plastic garages. £300

998 Bristol Britannia CANADIAN PACIFIC
Airliner, red stripe window panels, mint in
excellent later type illustrated box.
Sold for £220 Special Auction Services

701 Short Shetland Flying Boat, registration
G-AGVD, fair unboxed condition.
Sold for £130 Special Auction Services

Ref.	First Issued	Model	TPG

CARAVANS

30g	1936	**Caravan,** various 2-tone colours with white tyres. Unboxed.	
		Cream/blue	£120
		2-tone green	£120
		Cream/red	£120
		2-tone brown	£180
		Cream/yellow	£40
117	1963	**4 Berth Caravan** (formerly 188), yellow/cream & blue/cream versions. Yellow picture box	£30
188	1961	**4 Berth Caravan** (replaced by 117), blue/cream & green/cream versions. Yellow picture box	£30
190	1956	**Streamlined Caravan.** Yellow picture box with inner packing ring.........................	
		Blue/cream	£35
		Yellow/cream	£35

AIRCRAFT

The scale of early model aircraft varies greatly with most of the early models being approx 1:200 scale giving a typical wingspan of upto 5 inches, although some smaller aircraft are as little as 2 inches. As with other pre-war models, these suffered badly from metal fatigue so the price guide for these models is based on good condition as mint examples are nearly impossible to find. Similar to early ships, the 60 Aircraft Series were supplied unboxed or as part of gift sets

60a	**1934**	**Imperial Airways Liner** (later renumbered 66a), 4, 2-bladed propellers, with or without G-ABTI registration several colour variations. Unboxed	
		Blue	£440
		Gold	£220
		Gold & blue sunray wing design	£1,700

The model is presumed to be based on one of eight Armstrong Whitworth Atlantas in existence at the time which had had 4 engines yet seating for only 9 passengers. They were used on Nairobi to Cape Town and Karachi to Singapore routes.

60b	1934	**De Havilland Leopard Moth** (renumbered 66a), G-ACPT reg., green. Unboxed.	
		* Increase price guide by £100 for versions without registration	£130-150
60c	1934	**Percival Gull Monoplane** (later renumbered 60k), with or without G-ADZO registration, various colours, no PERCIVAL GULL under wing. Unboxed....................................	£60-90
60c	1934	Percival Gull Monoplane (later renumbered 60c), G-ADZO registration, various colours, PERCIVAL GULL under wing. Unboxed..	£150-200
		Souvenir model of the plane flown by Amy Mollinson on a return flight to Cape Town and exclusively boxed for the John Lewis store in Liverpool....................................	£280

Pair of 60s camouflaged Medium Bombers,
fair condition in a good early blue box.
Sold for £240 Special Auction Services

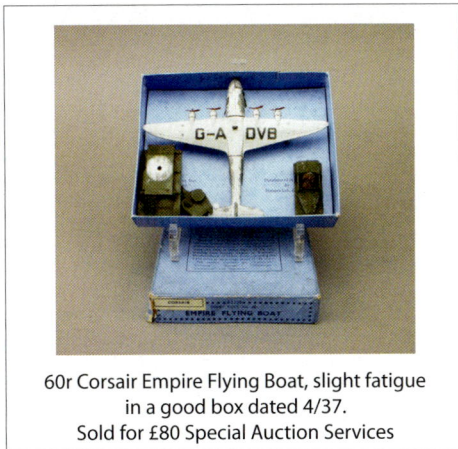

60r Corsair Empire Flying Boat, slight fatigue
in a good box dated 4/37.
Sold for £80 Special Auction Services

60d	1934	**Low Wing Monoplane** (later renumbered 66d), with or without G-AVYP registration, various colours. Unboxed £80-100
60e	1934	**General Monospa** (later renumbered 66e), with or without G-ABVP registration, various colours. Unboxed..£80-100
60f	1934	**Cierva Autogiro** (later renumbered 66f), cast-in pilot, gold/blue & silver/red versions. Unboxed.
		Gold with blue trim & rotors £150
		Silver with red trim £220
60g	1935	**De Havilland Comet,** G-ACSR reg., red, gold & silver versions. Unboxed..........................£60-80
60g	1945	**Light Racer,** G-RACE reg., red, silver & yellow versions. Unboxed £50-70
60h	1936	**Singapore Flying Boat,** silver. Blue printed box £120-150
60k	1936	**Percival Gull Amy Mollinson** (formerly 60c), G-ADZO reg., blue/silver. Yellow printed box.£250
60k	1936	Percival Gull Brook (formerly 60c), G-ADZO reg., blue/silver. Yellow printed box £110
60k	1936	Percival Gull Light Tourer (formerly 60c), unregistered. Unboxed £40
60m	1936	**4 Engined Flying Boat,** 4, 2-bladed propellers. Unboxed £150-180
		Blue G-EVCU registration £1,100
		Red G-EXGF registration £280
		Green G-EYCE registration £110
60n	1937	**Fairey Bomber** (later renumbered 60s), silver. Unboxed £60
		Supplied in blue printed trade boxes of 6. Price for a complete trade box £220
60p	1936	**Gloster Gladiator,** silver. Unboxed £60
60r	1937	**Empire Flying Boat** (later renumbered 60x), silver in various liveries. Unboxed versions....£50-60
		CALEDONIA in blue printed box..£170
		CLIO in blue printed box £110
		CANOPUS in blue printed box £90
		CORSAIR in blue printed box £90
		CANBERRA in blue printed box..£120
60s	1938	**Medium Bomber** (formerly 60n), camouflage version. Unboxed £40-50
60s	1940	**Fairey Bomber** (formerly 60n), camouflage version. Unboxed..........................£40-50
60t	1938	**Douglas DC3 Air Liner,** PH-ALI registration. Blue printed box £60-70
60v	1937	**Armstrong Whitworth Bomber,** camouflage & silver versions. Blue printed box £60-70
60w	1938	**Flying Boat Clipper III,** registration USA NC16736, silver. Blue printed box..........................£160

62p Armstrong Whitworth EXPLORER Air Liner, blue/silver, registration G-ADSV, good unboxed. Sold for £110 Special Auction Services

62t Armstrong Whitley Bomber, camouflage version, mint boxed complete with gliding wire & hook. Sold for £130 Wallis & Wallis

Ref.	First Issued	Model	TPG
60w	1945	**Flying Boat,** no markings, blue, green & silver versions. Unboxed	£45
60x	1937	**Atlantic Flying Boat** (formerly 60r),G-AZBP reg., lt blue/cream, 4 propellers. Unboxed.	£700
		* A very rare model and extremely difficult find in any condition	
62a	1939	**Vickers Supermarine Spitfire,** silver. Unboxed	£25-30
		Supplied to retailers in trade boxes of 6. Price for a complete trade box	£380
	1941	Meccano Spitfire Fund issue where the proceeds went to purchase a Spitfire for the M.O.D. within Souvenir box	£380
62b	1939	**Bristol Blenheim Bomber,** silver & camouflage versions. Unboxed	£20-25
62b	1945	**Medium Bomber,** silver. Unboxed	£20-25
62e	1940	**Vickers Supermarine Spitfire,** camouflage. Unboxed	£20-25
62g	1939	**Boeing Flying Fortress,** silver. Blue printed box	£70-80
62g	1945	**Long Range Bomber,** silver. Unboxed	£40-50
62h	1938	**Hawker Hurricane Fighter,** camouflaged.	£80-100
		Supplied to retailers in trade boxes of 6 strung and arranged in a gift set format. Price for complete box of 6	£1,400
62k	1938	**The King's Aeroplane,** silver/red/violet, G-AEXX registration. Blue printed box with 2 gliding instruction sheets	£150
62m	1938	**Airspeed Envoy Monoplane,** various registrations. Unboxed	£70-90
62m	1945	**Light Transport plane,** G-ATMH registration, blue, red, silver & blue versions. Unboxed	£50-60
62n	1938	**Junkers Ju90 Air Liner,** D-AALU, D-ADLH, D-AIVI & D-AURE reg., silver. Unboxed	£100-120
62p	1938	**Ensign Class Air Liner,** silver in various liveries. Blue printed box	£110-130
62p	1945	**Armstrong Whitworth Air liner,** G-ADTB & G-ADSV registrations, blue, green & silver versions. Blue printed box	£110-130
62r	1939	**DH Albatross Mail Liner,** G-AEVV registration, silver. Blue printed box	£110-130
62r	1945	**4 Engined Liner,** with or without G-ATPV registration, silver, grey & blue versions. Blue printed box	£110-130
62s	1939	**Hawker Hurricane Fighter,** silver. Unboxed	£50-70
62t	1939	**Armstrong Whitley Bomber** (formerly 60v), camouflage, leaflet. Blue printed box	£110-130

63 Mayo Composite Aircraft with 2 gliding clips and instructions, good in VG box dated 8.38.
Sold for £120 Special Auction Services

60m Four-Engined Flying Boat, red, registration G-EXGF, red plastic roller and green propellers.
Sold for £95 Special Auction Services

62w	1939	**Frobisher Class Air Liner** (formerly 68b), G-AFDJ, G-AFDK & G-AFDI registrations, silver. Blue printed box £90-110
62x	1939	**British 40 Seater Airliner** (later renumbered 68a), G-AZCA registration, various 2-tone colour versions. Blue printed box £110-130
62y	1939	**Giant High Speed Monoplane,** D-AZBK & D-ATVK registrations. Dk green......................£160 Silver......................£60 Lt Blue......................£190 Yellow......................£400 Blue/yellow, B-AZBK registration......................£180-200
63	1939	**Mayo Composite Aircraft** comprising 63a Flying Boat & 62b Seaplane. Blue printed box...£100-125 The real MERCURY Seaplane would hitch a lift with the MAIA Flying Boat before parting company to deliver long distance mail that could not be reached by MAIA.
63a	1939	**MAIA Flying Boat,** G-ADHK registration, silver. Unboxed £50-60
63b	1939	**MERCURY Seaplane,** G-ADHJ registration, silver. Unboxed £50-60
63b	1945	**Seaplane,** G-AKVW registration, silver. Unboxed ....£20-30 Supplied to retailers in trade boxes of 6. Price for a single model in a trade box £120
66a	1940	**Heavy Bomber** (formerly 60a), camouflage. Unboxed......................£200
66b	1940	**Dive Bomber Fighter** (formerly 60b), camouflage. Unboxed £320
66c	1940	**2 Seater Fighter** (formerly 60c), camouflage. Unboxed......................£460
66d	1940	**Torpedo Dive Bomber** (formerly 60d), camouflage. Unboxed £220
66e	1940	**Medium Bomber** (formerly 60e), camouflage. Unboxed......................£400
66f	1940	**Army Co-operation Autogiro** (formerly 60f), silver. Unboxed......................£220
67a	1940	**Junkers Ju89 Heavy Bomber,** black/blue version. Blue printed box......................£240
68a	1940	**Ensign Air Liner,** camouflage. Unboxed £500
68b	1940	**Frobisher Class Air Liner** (formerly 62w), camouflage. Unboxed......................£120-150
70a	1946	**Avro York Airliner** (later renumbered 704), G-AGJC registration, silver. Yellow printed box....£50-60
70b	1946	**Tempest II Fighter** (later renumbered 730), silver. Unboxed £20-25
70c	1947	**Viking Air Liner** (renumbered 705), G-AGOL registration, grey & silver versions. Unboxed .£30-40
70d	1946	**Twin Engined Fighter** (later renumbered 731), silver. Unboxed £25-30

722 Hawker Harrier Jump Jet, mint in near mint blister pack. Sold for £75 Aston's

719 Battle of Britain Spitfire Mk2, VG complete with instructions, decals, packing piece and batteries in a fair box. Sold for £50 Special Auction Services

Ref.	First Issued	Model	TPG
70e	1946	**Gloster Meteor** (later renumbered 732), silver. Unboxed £30-35	
70f	1947	**Lockheed Shooting Star** (later renumbered 733), silver with US star. Unboxed £25-30	
700	1954	**Seaplane** (formerly 63b), G-AVKW registration, silver. Unboxed £40-50	
700	1979	**Spitfire Mark II 'RAF Diamond Jubilee'**, chrome plated. Blue picture box........................£60-80	
701	1949	**Short Shetland Flying Boat,** G-AGVD registration. Unboxed. £120	
		Models in rare plain brown card box with orange / white label £680	
702	1954	**DH Comet BOAC Jet Airliner,** G-ALYV reg., white / blue. Blue / white striped box............£80-100	
704	1954	**Avro York Airliner** (formerly 70a), G-AGJC reg., silver. Yellow printed box £70-90	
705	1952	**Viking Air Liner** (formerly 70c), G-AGOL reg., silver. Yellow printed box............................£50-60	
706	1956	**Vickers Viscount Airliner AIR FRANCE,** F-BGNL reg., silver / blue / white. Yellow picture box .£30-40	
708	1957	**Vickers Viscount Airliner BEA,** G-AOJA reg., silver / white & grey / white versions. Yellow	
		picture box £50-60	
710	1965	**Beechcraft S35 Bonanza,** red / white, red / blue & brown / yellow versions. Colour picture	
		box & bubble packed on tray £35-45	
		German promotional: GLUCK MIT WICKULER livery in plain white box £280	
712	1972	**US Army T42A,** green. Colour picture box & bubble packed on tray £50-60	
715	1956	**Bristol 173 Helicopter,** G-AUXR registration, lt blue. Yellow picture box £50-60	
715	1968	**Beechcraft Baron C55,** red / yellow & white / yellow versions. Colour picture box. £30-40	
716	1957	**Westland S51 Sikorsky Helicopter,** red / cream. Yellow picture box £35-45	
717	1970	**Boeing 737 LUFTHANSA Jumbo Jet,** blue / white. Bubble pack £35-45	
718	1972	**Hawker Hurricane MkIIC,** camouflage. Bubble pack £40-50	
719	1969	**Spitfire MkII** (later renumbered 741) with motorised propellor, camouflage. Colour	
		'Battle of Britain picture box & bubble packed versions. £65-75	
721	1969	**Junkers JU87B Stuka with bomb,** grey / yellow. Colour 'Battle of Britain' picture box &	
		bubble packed on tray. Reduce price guide by £20 for window box version.................................£60	
722	1970	**Hawker Harrier, camoflauge.** Colour picture box & bubble packed on tray.............................£70	
723	1970	**Hawker Siddeley HS125,** yellow / blue / white & blue / white versions. Bubble pack.................£35	

Rare 828 Avro Vulcan Delta Wing Bomber, one of only 500 produced in 1955-56, casting flaws otherwise excellent. Sold for £700 Wallis & Wallis

726 Messerschmitt 109E mint bubble pack complete with instructions.
Sold for £165 Special Auction Services

724	1971	**Sea King Helicopter** with space capsule, blue/white. Colour picture card box	£50
725	1972	**Royal Navy Phantom II,** blue. Bubble packed	£75
		20x15cm window poster for above model. Sold in 2006	£40
726	1972	**Messerschmitt BF109E,** decal sheets. Bubble packed	
		Desert camouflage	£60
		Military Green, yellow nose version with battery driven propeller	£180
727	1976	**USAF Phantom FK MkII,** 2 missiles, 2 figures, brown/olive camouflauge. Bubble packed.	
		US issue	£360
728	1972	**RAF Dominie,** blue camouflage. Bubble packed	£35-45
729	1974	**Multi Role Combat Aircraft,** camouflage. Bubble packed	£35-45
730	1952	**Tempest II Fighter (formerly 70b),** silver. Yellow picture box	£30-40
703	1972	**US Navy SARATOGA Phantom II,** grey/red. Bubble packed	£75-85
731	1952	**Twin Engined Fighter** (formerly 70d), silver. Yellow picture box	£20-25
731	1973	**SEPECAT Jaguar,** opening cockpit, blue/camouflage. Bubble packed	£35-45
732	1952	**Gloster Meteor** (formerly 70e), silver. Yellow picture box	£20-25
732	1974	**Bell Police Helicopter with signs & cones,** orange/blue/white. Window box	£25-30
733	1952	**Lockheed Shooting Star** (formerly 70f), silver. Yellow picture box	£25-30
733	1973	**F4K Phantom II with 2 missiles,** brown, decal sheet.	
		Brown/green camouflage US version	£200
		German issue: Grey/green camouflage DER BUNDESLUFFWAFFE. Sold in 2005	£620
734	1955	**Supermarine Swift,** camouflage. Yellow picture box	£25-30
734	1975	**USAAF P47 Thunderbolt,** silver/black, decal sheet. Bubble pack	£80
735	1956	**Gloster Javelin,** camouflage. Yellow picture box	£35-45
736	1955	**Hawker Hunter,** camouflage. Yellow picture box	£25-30
736	1973	**Bundesmarine Sea King Helicopter,** grey/orange. Bubble packed	£35-45
737	1959	**P1B Lightning Fighter,** silver. Yellow picture box.	£35
738	1960	**De Havilland DH110 Sea Vixen ROYAL NAVY Fighter,** grey/white. Yellow picture box	£40-50
739	1975	**A6M5 Zero Sen,** battery operated, blue/black Japanese markings with decal sheet. Bubble pack	£70

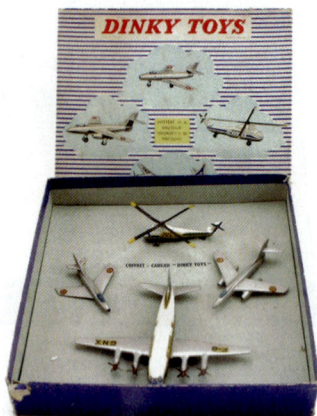

Set 60 Aeroplanes comprising
60A Daussault Mystere,
60B Vautour,
60D Sikorsky &
60E Vickers Viscount,
VG in excellent box.
Sold for £370
Special Auction Services

Ref.	First Issued	Model	TPG
741	1978	**Spitfire MkII (formerly 719) non motorised,** camouflage. Bubble pack & red/blue window box	£35-45
749	1955	**RAF AVRO Vulcan Bomber,** silver. Blue/white striped numbered 992	£1,700
		* Production problems experienced in casting the aluminium wings resulted in only 500 examples being made to fulfil a Canadian order. Thanks to Wallis & Wallis for this information.	
997	1962	**Caravelle SE210 AIR FRAINCE Air Liner,** silver/blue/white version. Yellow & blue/white stripe lift off lid box versions	£90-110
998	1959	**CANADIAN PACIFIC Bristol Britannia,** CF-CZA registration, silver/blue/white & silver grey versions. Blue/white striped lift off lid box	£140-160
999	1955	**DH Comet Jet Airliner** (formerly 702), G-ALYV registration, white/blue version. Blue/white stripe & yellow lift off lid box versions	£80-100
-	1979	**RAF Nimrod.** Only 30 were produced (with and without bulbous noses) but not released after the Dinky factory went into liquidation 1979. Packaged in plain white boxes or blue cellophane packs together with numbered certificate.	£120-150

GIFT SETS

60	1934	**Aeroplane Set;** 60a Imperial, 60b Leopard Moth, 60c Percival Gull, 60d Monoplane, 60e Monospar, & 60f Autogiro. Blue label box	£800
60p	1938	**6pce Gloster Gladiator Set.** Blue printed label box	£300
60s	1938	**2pce Fairey Bomber Set.** Blue printed label box	£170
61	1937	**RAF Aeroplane Set;** 60h Singapore Flying Boat, 2 x 60n Fairy Bombers & 2 x 60p Biplanes. Blue printed box	£2,200
62d	1939	**6pce Bristol Blenheim Bomber Set.** Green label box	£380
62e	1939	**5pce Spitfire set.** Blue printed box	£380
62s	1939	**6pce Hawker Hurricane Fighter Set.** Blue printed box	£1,400
64	1939	**Aeroplane Set;** 60g Racer, 62h Hurricane, 62k Kings Aeroplane, 62m Light Transport, 62s Hurrican & 63b Seaplane. Blue label box	£1,200
66	1940	**Aeroplane Set;** 66a Bomber, 66b Dive Bomber Fighter, 66c Fighter, 66d Torpedo, 66e Bomber & 66f Autogiro. Yellow/brown label box	£1750-2250
68	1939	**Aeroplane Set;** 2x60s Fairey Bombers, 2x62d Blenheims, 3x62h Hurricanes, 3x62e Spitfire, 62t Armstrong Bomber, 68a Armstrong Airliner & 68b Frobisher. Blue picture label box	£2,500
		This 13pce set is the rarest of all Dinky pre-war aircraft sets	

Pre-war group comprising 2 Cunard White
Star Liners and 12 Battleships, fair condition
all with degrees of fatigue.
Sold for £55 Special Auction Services

796 Healey Sports Boat, green/cream on orange
trailer, mint in excellent gold double ended
window box for export market.
Sold for £45 Special Auction Services

BOATS, SHIPS & HOVERCRAFT

The early '50's Series' range of ships were cast from an unstable alloy, used on many of the early Dinky toys, resulting in metal fatigue problems. They were sold unboxed by retailers or as a part of gift sets. The price guide refers to mint examples (with boxes where applicable).

50a	1934	**Battle Cruiser HMS Hood,** grey. Unboxed	£20-25
50b	1934	**Battleship HMS Nelson,** grey. Unboxed	£20-25
50b	1934	**Battleship HMS Rodney,** grey. Unboxed	£20-25
50c	1934	**Cruiser HMS Effingham,** grey. Unboxed	£20-25
50d	1934	**Cruiser HMS York,** grey. Unboxed	£20-25
50e	1934	**Cruiser HMS Delhi,** grey. Unboxed	£20-25
50f	1934	**Destroyer Broke Class,** grey. Unboxed	£8-12
50g	1935	**Submarine K Class,** grey. Unboxed	£8-12
50h	1935	**Destroyer Amazon Class,** grey. Unboxed	£8-12
50k	1935	**Submarine X Class,** grey. Unboxed	£8-12
50m	-	**A bronze prototype of aircraft carrier HMS Ark Royal,** originally intended for production in 1941 but discouraged from being made by the government and the interuption of Dinky's factory being turned over to wartime production, resulting in the model never being made	£3000
51b	1934	**Norddeutscher-Lloyd Europa,** black/white. Unboxed	£25-30
51c	1935	**Italia Line Rex,** black/white. Unboxed	£25-30
51d	1934	**CPR Empress of Britain,** blue. Unboxed	£20-25
51e	1935	**P&O Strathaird,** white. Unboxed	£20-25
51f	1934	**Furness-Withy Line Queen of Bermuda,** grey/white. Unboxed	£20-25
51g	1934	**Cunard White Star Liner Brittanic,** black/white. Unboxed	£20-25
52	1934	**Cunard Liner No 534,** black/white/red. Unboxed	£65-75
52a	1935	**Cunard Liner Queen Mary,** black/white/red. Blue picture label box	£80-90
52b	1935	**Cunard Queen Mary,** black/red/white. Blue picture label box	£80-90
52c	1935	**La Normandie,** black/white (made in France). Blue picture label box	£50-60
52m	1936	**Cunard Queen Mary,** black/red/white. Blue picture label box	£80-90

Rare yellow 282 Duple Roadmaster Coach
with red coach lines and green hubs,
good condition, parts fair with some chipping.
Sold by Special Auction Services

29e Single Deck Bus, cream with blue flash,
black ridged hubs, mint unboxed.
Sold for £100 DJ Auctions

Ref.	First Issued	Model	TPG
53az	1938	**Battleship Dunkerque,** grey (made in France). Picture lid box	£40-50
281	1973	**Military Hovercraft,** red. Yellow/red/blue header window box	£15-20
290	1970	**SRN-6 Hovercraft,** red with black or blue skirt. Colour picture box	£25-30
671	1976	**Mk1 Corvette,** brown/white/black/grey with missiles. Window box	£20-25
672	1976	**OSA-Missile Boat** white/black/grey with missiles. Window box	£20-25
673	1977	**Submarine Chaser,** white/grey/black with depth chargers. Window box	£20-25
674	1977	**Coastguard Missile Launch,** blue/white/red/yellow with missiles. Window box	£20-25
675	1973	**Motor Patrol Boat,** grey. Window box	£20-25
		Pre-production bare metal casting with plastic fittings sold in 2009	£35
678	1974	**Air Sea Rescue Launch with dinghy,** grey/black/yellow. Window box	£20-25
796	1960	**Healy Sports Boat & Trailer,** orange trailer, black plastic wheels unless stated. Yellow box.	£50-60
		Green/cream	£50
		Red/cream	£70
		Red/cream (grey wheel version)	£110
		Yellow/cream	£90
		Yellow/cream (grey wheel version)	£200
		Double ended export window box containing red/gream boat. Sold in 2008	£110
797	1966	**Healy Sports Boat (no trailer),** yellow, red & cream versions. Unboxed supplied in	
		Trade Box of 6's	£30-40
		Supplied in trade box of 6. Sold in 2009	£280

GIFT SETS

50	1934	**Ships of the British Navy;** 50a Hood, 50b Nelson, 50b Rodney, 50c Effingham, 50d York, 50e Delhi, 3 x 50f Broke, 50g Submarine, 3 x 50h Amazon & 50k Submarine. Blue box with colour label	£400
51	1934	**Great Liners Set;** 51b Europa, 51d Empress of Britain, 51e Strathaird, 51f Bermuda, 51g Britannia. Blue box with colour label	£320

29f Observation Coach & 29e Single Deck Bus, both VG unboxed. Sold for £160 Wallis & Wallis

BUSES & COACHES

29	1934	**Motor Bus, MARMITE logo.** Unboxed	
		Red/cream with repainted roof	£280
		Yellow/silver	£400
		Cream/maroon with repainted roof	£110
		Green/cream	£480
		Supplied to retailers in trade boxes of 6. Price for complete trade box with 6 models	£1,400
29b	1936	**Streamlined Bus,** mid blue/dk blue, mid green/dk green, silver/red & grey/blue. Unboxed	£40-60
		Cream, blue roof & wheel covers	£150
		Red, maroon roof & wheel covers	£280
29c	1938	**Double Decker Bus,** DUNLOP TYRES, early advertising version with cream roof in various colours. Unboxed	£140-160
		Supplied to retailers in trade boxes of 6. Price for a single model in a trade box	£200
29c	1946	Double Decker Bus (without advertising). Unboxed	£100-120
29c	1954	Double Decker Bus, DUNLOP - The World's Master Tyre, later advertising version with cream roof in various colours. Unboxed	£70-90
29e	1948	**Single Deck Bus,** various colours with flashes. Yellow picture box	£45-60
		* Add £50 to price guide for green hub version	
29f	1950	**Observation Coach,** various colours with flashes. Unboxed	£60-70
		Supplied to retailers in trade boxes of 6. Price for complete trade box with 6 models	£400
29g	1951	**Luxury Coach** (renumbered 281). Unboxed unless stated	
		Maroon, cream side stripe, maroon or red hubs	£100
		Mid blue, cream side stripe, yellow hubs	£240
		Cream, orange side stripe, cream hubs	£100
		Fawn, orange side stripe, cream hubs	£110
		* Add £50 to price guide for models sold in yellow 29g/281 dual numbered boxes	
29h	1952	**Duple Roadmaster Coach.** Unboxed	
		Green/cream	£160
		Dk red, silver trim	£30
		Dk blue, silver trim	£25
		Trade box containing 6 models. Sold in 2008	£240
		* Add £30 to Price guide for models sold in yellow 282/29h dual numbered boxes	
31	1939	**Holland Coach Craft Van.** Unboxed	
		Green	£130
		Orange	£160
		Violet Blue	£240
		Yellow	£200

Rare pre-war 31 orange version Holland Coachcraft Van, slight fatigue, no box. Sold for £780 Special Auction Services

Scarce Promotional 289 FORDATH Routemaster Bus, mint boxed. Sold for £80 Wallis & Wallis

Ref.	First Issued	Model	TPG
280	1954	**Observation Coach,** later renumbering of 29f, various colours with flashes. Yellow dual numbered picture box	£80-90
281	1954	**Luxury Coach,** later renumbering of 29g, various colours with flashes	£140-160
		* Add £50 to price guide for scarce yellow & green hub versions	
282	1954	**Duple Roadmaster Coach,** later renumbering of 29h, various colours	£80-100
		* Add £30 to price guide for scarce yellow version.	
283	1956	**BOAC Coach,** blue/white, white or black tyres. Red/yellow or yellow picture box versions	£55-65
283	1971	**Single Deck Bus,** red. Card box & bubble pack versions	£40-50
289	1964	**Routemaster Bus,** various advertising promotional decals. Window box unless stated	
	1964	TERN SHIRTS, red. Yellow picture box	£40
	1966	SCHWEPPES, red. Picture box	£50
	1969	ESSO, red. Picture box, bubble pack & window box versions	£30
	1970	ESSO, silver version in window box	£60
	1968	FESTIVAL of LONDON STORES, red. Picture box	£50
	1970	INGERSOLL RAND, red	£40
	1977	MADAME TUSSAUDS, blue. Picture box & bubble pack versions	£60
	1970	WOOLWORTHS, silver	£50
	1970	EVER READY, silver	£70
	1970	DINKY TOYS, red	£80
	1970	NESTLES, gold	£70
	1979	SHOPLINKER, yellow/red	£100
	1979	THOLLEMBEEK, silver (Belgium promotional)	£70
	1979	FORDATH, red. White box	£100
	1979	GREENLINE JUBILEE, red	£40
	1979	BLACKPOOL ZOO, cream	£50
	1979	10th ANNIVERSARY of the NEW ZEALAND MODEL CAR CLUB, red	£90
290	1954	**Double Decker Bus,** later renumbering of 29c, DUNLOP decal, red or green versions with cream roof. Yellow picture box.	£80
		* Add £40 to price guide for other colour versions	
291	1961	**London Bus,** EXIDE BATTERIES, route 73, ridged or plain metal hubs. Yellow card box	
		Green/cream	£120
		Red	£60
		Chloride Batteries promotional in red with 'Exide Brand Advertising' information slip.	£140

952 Vega Major Luxury Coach, white with burgundy stripe, good in a worn box. Sold for £50 Aston's

291 Leyland EXIDE BATTERIES London Bus, mint in VG yellow pictorial box. Sold for £70 Wallis & Wallis

291	1974	**Atlantean City Bus,** Speedwheels. Bubble pack (unless stated)	
		KENNINGS, orange	£20
		KENNINGS, white	£30
		YELLOW PAGES, silver. Window box	£100
		ESSO, red	£20
	1977	LONDON & MANCHESTER ASSURANCE, white. Limited edition of 50 in plain card box. Sold in 2002	£860
292	1962	**Atlantean City Bus,** RIBBLE decal, red/white. Red/yellow picture box	£50-70
	1963	**Atlantean City Bus,** BP decal, red/white. Red/yellow picture box	£60-80
293	1973	**Swiss Postal Bus PTT,** yellow, cream roof. Bubble pack	£20-30
		20x15cm window poster for above model. Sold in 2006	£30
295	1963	**Atlas Kenebrake Bus,** lt blue. Yellow picture box.	£40-50
295	1973	**Atlantean Bus,** YELLOW PAGES, yellow. Bubble packed	£25-35
296	1972	**Duple Viceroy 37 Coach,** blue or yellow/crean versions. Bubble packed	£25-35
297	1977	**Silver Jubilee Bus,** NATIONAL decal, silver/black. Window box	£20-30
	1977	**Silver Jubilee Bus,** WOOLWORTHS decal, silver. Window box	£20-30
949	1961	**Wayne School Bus,** yellow with red stripe.	
		Blue/white stripe lift-off lid box	£80
		Colour picture lift-off lid box containing with black stripe model	£120
952	1964	**Vega Major Luxury Coach,** grey & white versions. Picture box	£45-55
953	1963	**Continental Touring Coach,** blue with white roof. Lift off picture lid box	£150-170
954	1972	**Vega Major Luxury Coach,** white with purple stripe, light & dark blue interior versions	
		Colour picture box with end flaps	£60
		Bubble pack version	£40
961	1973	**Swiss Postal Bus,** yellow, red stripe, cream roof with 2 roof lights, PTT decal.	
		Illustrated Colour box (standard issue)	£100
		Swiss issue: AUTOCAR POSTAL box. Sold in 2006	£220

GIFT SETS

300	1973	**London Scene Set;** 289 Routemaster & 284 Taxi. Window box	£35

Early 36g Taxi (1947) in red, VG unboxed. Sold for £115 Wallis & Wallis

TAXI'S

36g	1936	**Taxi with Driver,** black smooth rounded hubs, white or black tyres, black roof to all. Unboxed
		Yellow / black £520
		Violet blue / black £300
		Grey / black £70
		Red / black £280
		Supplied in trade boxes of 6. Single model in a trade box sold in 2008 ....£320
36g	1947	**Taxi with Driver,** black ridged hubs, black tyres, black roof to all. Unboxed.
		Dark green £45
		Light green..£70
		Maroon..£40
		Red £170
		Supplied in trade boxes of 6. Single model in a trade box sold in 2010 ....£70
40h	1952	**Austin FX3 Taxi** (renumbered 254), cast driver, yellow. Unboxed
		Dark blue £120
		Green / yellow £70
		Violet blue £200
		Yellow £70
		Empty trade box for 6 models. Sold in 2009 ....£140
115	1979	**United Biscuits Taxi,** yellow / blue / black. Plain white promotional model £20
120	1979	**Happy Cab,** 'Flower Power' stickers. Window box..£35-45
241	1977	**Silver Jubilee Taxi,** Union Jack decal on boot. Window box...£15
254	1956	**Austin Taxi** (formerly 40h), black & 2-tone yellow / green versions. Yellow picture box........£65-80
		* Add £150 to price guide for blue & yellow versions
265	1960	**Plymouth Taxi** (USA), 25c decal, yellow / red. Yellow picture box £125-150
266	1960	**Plymouth Taxi** (Canadian), 450 Metro Cab decal, yellow / red. Yellow picture box £90-110
268	1962	**Renault Dauphine Mini Cab,** MECCANO, KENWOOD & BRITAX decals, red.
		Red / yellow box £90-110
278	1978	**Plymouth Yellow Cab with decal.** Window box £15
		DETROIT CITY CAB CO., yellow / orange pre-production modelSold in 2008 ....£110
282	1967	**Austin 1800 Taxi,** blue / white with TAXI decals on doors & roof. Picture box........................£50-60
284	1972	**London Taxi,** black & dk blue versions. Window box..£25-35
		20x15cm window poster for above model. Sold in 2006 ....£40

30f Ambulance, grey, open windows, black chassis, black smooth hubs, excellent unboxed. Sold for £60 DJ Auctions

Selection of emergency accessories, 12 pieces in good condition. Sold for £45 Toy Price Guide archive

EMERGENCY - AMBULANCE

24a	1934	**Ambulance,** cream & grey versions with white tyres. Unboxed.
		Cream 1st type (criss-cross chassis) £600
		Cream or grey 2nd type (open criss-cross chassis) £120
		Grey 2nd type...£240
30f	1935	**Ambulance,** grey & cream versions. Unboxed £130-160
		Supplied to retailers in trade boxes of 6. Price for a single model in a trade box £190
30h	1950	**Daimler Ambulance** (later renumbered 253), cream with red cross. Unboxed.
		* Add £50 for green US market version
		Cream £20
		White £30
		Military green version...£60
		Trade box containing 4 cream models. Sold in 2009...£150
263	1962	**Superior Criterion Ambulance,** white, stretcher & patient. Yellow/red picture box £45
267	1967	**Superior Cadillac Ambulance,** cream, stretcher & patient, roof light. Colour picture box £70
267	1978	**Paramedic Truck,** red, 2 plastic figures, 'Emergency' badge. Window box £25-35
268	1973	**Range Rover Ambulance,** stretcher, white. Bubble pack...£25-35
276	1976	**Ford Transit Ambulance,** white. Window box £30-35
277	1962	**Superior Criterion Ambulance,** flashing roof light, blue. Colour lift-off lid box £80
278	1964	**Vauxhall Victor Ambulance,** stretcher, white. Yellow/red picture box £90
288	1971	**Superior Cadillac Ambulance,** stretcher & patient, white version without flashing roof light.
		Colour picture box...45-55
		White/yellow pre-production variation (part of an unreleased 2pce gift set)...........................£240
		MANHATTAN BEACH FIRE DEPT. Unusual decal version. Window box. £15

955 Commer Fire Engine, VG in good yellow picture box. Sold for £55 Toy Price Guide archive

258 Desoto Fireflite USA Police Car, good condition in a fair box. Sold for £45 Special Auction Services

EMERGENCY - FIRE

25h	1936	**Streamlined Fire Engine** (later renumbered 250), red, black or white tyres. Unboxed.	£120
		Trade boxes for 6 models containing one example. Sold in 2009	£140
25k	1937	**Streamlined Fire Engine** with bell & 6 firemen, red with white tyres. Unboxed.	£190
250	1954	**Streamline Fire Engine** (formerly 25h), red. Yellow picture box	£75-95
253	1954	**Daimler Ambulance** (formerly 30h), cream or white versions, red cross. Yellow picture box	£70
259	1961	**Bedford Fire Engine,** red. Yellow picture box	£60-70
263	1978	**ERF Airport Rescue Fire Tender,** yellow. Window box	£30-35
266	1976	**ERF Fire Tender,** red. Window box	£30-40
267	1978	**Unissued red pre-production model** with FORESTRY FIRE DEFENCE DEPT. decal eventually released as a Paramedic Truck	£70
271	1975	**Fire Ford Transit,** red. Bubble pack	£65
276	1962	**Airport Fire Tender** with bell, red. Yellow lift-off lid picture box.	£80
282	1973	**Land Rover Fire Appliance,** red with metal ladder. Window box	£25-30
285	1969	**Merryweather Marquis Fire Tender,** lred, adder, pump. Colour picture box	£60-70
286	1968	**Ford Transit Fire Van with hose,** red. Colour picture box & bubble packs	£35-45
384	1977	**Fire Rescue Wagon.** Window box	£15-20
410	1974	**Bedford CF FIRE RESCUE UNIT,** CODE 3 applied decals, silver ladder, Speedwheels. Window box	£30
		As above with FALCK CODE 3 decals. Window box	£45
555 & 955	1952-70	**Fire Engine** (renumbered 955), red, extending silver ladder, grey tyres on earlier issues later replaced by black tyres. Based on the Commer Carmichael fire engine built by the Hampshire Car Bodies company, the model (later renumbered 955) was first produced in 1952 with the last batch made in 1970, during which time the basic casting hardly changed, however with 9 model/packaging variations it gives a good indication of the subtle changes Dinky made to their popular models as follows:	
555	1952	Red, early tan ladder variation, open windows, blue lift-off lid box with orange/white label	£110
555	1953	Red, silver ladder, open windows, blue lift-off lid box with orange/white label	£150
555	1953	Red, silver ladder, open windows, 555 numbered blue/white stripe lift-off lid box	£75
555/ 955	1954	Red, silver ladder, open windows, 555 & 955 dual numbered blue/white stripe lift-off lid box	£75
555	1955	Red, silver ladder, open windows, 555 numbered blue/white stripe SUPERTOYS lift-off lid box	£75

753 Police Controlled Crossing, excellent and fully complete. Sold for £90 Toy Price Guide archive

270 AA Motorcycle Patrol with solid black knobbly tyres. Sold for £25 Toy Price Guide archive

Ref.	First Issued	Model	TPG
955	1957	Red, silver ladder, open windows, 955 numbered blue/white stripe lift-off lid box	£65
955	1961	Red, silver ladder, glazed windows, 955 numbered blue/white stripe lift-off lid box	£65
955	1964	Red, silver ladder, glazed windows, 955 numbered yellow/red picture lift-off lid box	£80
955	1966	Red, silver ladder, glazed windows, 955 numbered colour picture lift-off lid box	£90
		* The following changes were made over 18 years; 4 baseplate versions, 2 tow hook mounting versions & 2 bell types.	
956	1956	**Bedford Turntable Fire Escape,** ladder, red cab with silver, black or white turntable versions. Blue/white stripe lift-off lid box version	£70
956	1969	**Berliet Turntable Fire Escape,** ladder, red cab with silver, black or white turntable versions. Colour picture box version	£120-140

EMERGENCY - POLICE

195	1971	**Fire Chief's Range Rover,** Speedwheels, red. Colour picture box	£20-25
243	1979	**Volvo Police Car,** white. Window box	£25-30
		Blue/white POLITI Pre-production model	£160
244	1977	**Plymouth Fury Police Car,** black/white. Window box	£25-30
		Pre-Production model in blue/white with POLICE DEPT. decals	£150
250	1967	**Police Mini Cooper S,** white, roof sign, aerial. Colour picture box	£45-55
251	1971	**USA Pontiac Parisienne Police Car,** white, roof siren & light, 2 aerials. Colour picture box	£120
252	1969	**ROYAL CANADIAN MOUNTED POLICE Pontiac Police Car,** blue with white doors, red roof light, 2 aerials. Colour picture box	£50-60
254	1971	**Police Range Rover,** white, orange stripes, 2 aerials, Speedwheels. Colour picture box	£40-50
255	1955	**MERSEY TUNNEL Police Land Rover Van,** red. Yellow picture box	£40
255	1967	**Ford Zodiac Police Car,** white, aerial & roof sign. Colour picture box	£50
255	1977	**Police Mini Clubman,** blue/white, plastic wheels. Window box	£20
256	1960	**Humber Hawk Police Car,** black, driver & passenger, roof sign. Yellow picture box	£50
257	1960	**Canadian Nash Rambler Fire Chief's Car,** red, roof light. Yellow picture box	£55
258	1960	**USA De Soto Fireflite Police Car,** black, white front doors, roof light. Yellow picture box	£50

Unboxed Dinky 37b Police Motorcyclist. Dark Blue Rider, Black Motorcycle and Black rubber wheels. Mint unboxed. Sold for £42, DJ Auctions

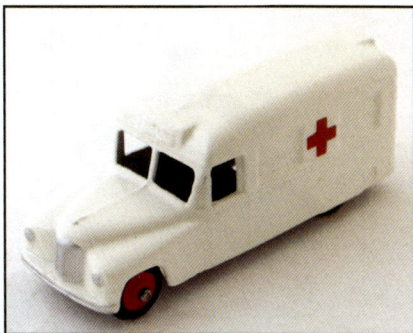

Unboxed Dinky 253 Daimler Ambulance. White, Red Cross Red ridged hubs. Mint unboxed. Sold for £50, DJ Auctions

258	1961	**USA Dodge Royal Police Car,** black, white front doors, roof light. Yellow picture box..............£50
258	1966	**USA Ford Fairlane Police Car,** black or blue/white versions, white front doors, red roof light. Yellow picture box..£50
258	1966	**USA Cadillac Police Car,** black/white. Yellow picture box...£50
264	1962	**ROYAL CANADIAN MOUNTED POLICE Ford Fairlane Police Car,** blue with white doors, aerial, red roof light. Gold export window box..£110
264	1965	**ROYAL CANADIAN MOUNTED POLICE Cadillac Police Car,** blue with white doors, aerial, red roof light. Yellow picture box..£40
264	1978	**Rover 3500 Police Car,** white with yellow stripe. Window box..£35
269	1962	**Jaguar Motorway Police Car,** 2 seated figures, aerial & blue roof light. Yellow picture box......£85
269	1978	**Ford Transit Police Van,** white/red/blue, plastic figures, cones & signs. Window box........£30-40
270	1969	**Ford Police Panda Car,** turquoise, roof sign, Speedwheels on later issues. Colour picture box...£40-50
272	1975	**Police Accident Unit,** white, roof radar, aerial, cones & signs. Bubble pack............................£40-50
274	1978	**Ford Transit Ambulance,** white. Window box...£20
277	1977	**Police Land Rover,** black, blue roof light. Window box..£25-35
287	1967	**Police Accident Unit,** white, roof sign, radar, aerial, white with orange panels. Colour picture box. £50
956	956	**Bedford Turntable Fire Escape,** ladder, red. Blue/white stripe Supertoy box...........................£75 * Add £50 to price guide for yellow lift-off lid picture box version
2253	2253	**Ford Capri Police Car** (1:25 scale), white/orange, roof light, Police decal. Bubble pack............£40

EMERGENCY GIFT SETS

008	1961	**Fire Station Staff** (35mm) plastic 6pce figure set. Sealed in clear plastic bag or yellow card box...£30
42	1937	**4pce Police Set** including; 42a tin plate Police Box, 42b Motor Cycle Patrol, 42c Police Guide directing traffic (white coat) & 42d Police Guide directing traffic (blue coat). Blue box with inner card diorama £240
294	1973	**Police Vehicles Set** (replaced 297); 250 Mini, 254 Range Rover & 287 Accident Unit. Picture box with diorama inner tray...£140
297	1963	**Police Vehicles Set** (replaced by 294); 250 Mini, 255 Zodiac & 287 Accident Unit. Picture box with diorama inner tray...£150

Unboxed Dinky # 37c Pre War Royal Signals Dispatch Rider. Khaki Rider, Green Motorcyclist and White rubber wheels. Good Totally restored to a very high standard unboxed. Sold for £20, DJ Auctions

Unboxed Dinky # 42b Police Motorcycle Patrol. Blue Rider, Black Motorcycle, Green Sidecar and Black rubber wheels. Mint unboxed. Sold for £55, DJ Auctions

Ref.	First Issued	Model	TPG
298	1963	**Emergency Services Set;** 258 Cadillac, 263 Ambulance, 276 Fire Tender & 277 Ambulance with 5 firemen, policeman & 2 ambulance attendants. Card box with inner card display tray £420	
299	1963	**Motorway Services Set;** 434 Crash Truck, 269 Police Car, 257 Fire Car, 276 Airport Tender & 263 Ambulance. Illustrated plain card lid with inner card display tray £1,700	
299	1978	**Crash Squad Action Set;** 244 Police Car & 732 Helicopter. Window box ....£45 Shrink wrapped trade pack of 6 boxed sets..£160	
304	1978	**Fire Rescue Gift Set;** 195 Range Rover, 282 Land Rover & 384 Truck. Window box..............£50-60	
957	1959	**Fire Services Set;** 257 Fire Chief's Car, 955 Fire Engine & 956 Turntable Fire Escape. Yellow lift-off lid picture box with yellow card insert £170	

Yellow Trade Box for 3/27B Harvest Trailer,
poor condition with grafitti.
Sold for £45 Special Auction Services

Dinky 343 Dodge Farm Produce Wagon. Green cab
and chassis, Yellow back and Yellow ridged hubs.
Mint in Very Good tape repaired correct colour
spot box. Sold for £120, DJ Auctions

FARM

22e	1933	**Farm Tractor,** HORNBY SERIES or DINKY TOYS cast inside, tow hook to some. 7 known colour variations all with red wheels. Supplied in Trade Box containing 6 models

Blue/cream chassis..£100
Cream/blue chassis..£110
Cream/red chassis...£120
Green/yellow chassis...£110
Red/blue chassis £60
Yellow/blue chassis £80
All yellow £240
Empty Trade Box for 6 models sold in 2010 ....£380

27a	1948	**Massey Harris Tractor** with driver (later renumbered 300), red, yellow metal wheels. Supplied in Trade Box for 3 models

Unboxed model...£30
Trade box with inner divisions containing 3 models. Sold in 2009 ....£130
Model in later dual numbered 27A/300 yellow illustrated box...£60

27b	1949	**Halesowen Harvest Trailer** (later renumbered 320), brown, red racks, metal wheels. Supplied in Trade Box for 3 models

Unboxed model...£20
Trade box with inner divisions containing 3 models £80

27c	1949	**Manure Spreader** (renumbered 321), red with silver shredders. Yellow picture box..................£30
27d	1950	**Land Rover** (later renumbered 340), orange & green versions. Yellow picture box £60-75
27g	1949	**Moto-Cart with driver** (later renumbered 342), brown/green. Yellow picture box £30
27h	1951	**Disc Harrow** (later renumbered 322), red/yellow. Unboxed £15
		Supplied to retailers in trade boxes of 4. Price for a single model in a trade box £120
27j	1952	**Triple Gang Mower** (later renumbered 323), red. Unboxed..£30
		Supplied to retailers in trade boxes of 3. Price for a single model in a trade box £150
27k	1953	**Hay Rake** (later renumbered 324), red. Yellow printed box £40-45
27m	1952	**Land Rover Trailer** (later renumbered 341), green, orange & red versions............................£25-30
		Trade box containing 4 trailers. Sold in 2007 ....£80
		Rare dark blue version (unboxed). Sold in 2008 ....£70
		* For trailers in yellow 27m/341 dual numbered card boxes add £20
27n	1953	**Field Marshall Tractor** with metal driver (formerly 27n), orange. Yellow picture box. £60

300 Massey Ferguson Tractor with plastic front hubs, mint in a creased picture box. Sold for £120 Warwick & Warwick

301 Field Marshall Tractor (sold for £50) and 308 Leyland Tractor (sold for £45), good condition in repro boxes. Sold by Special Auction Services

Ref.	First Issued	Model	TPG

Ref.	First Issued	Model	TPG
30n	1950	**Farm Produce Wagon** (later renumbered 343), red, green & yellow cab versions. Yellow picture box	£55
105a	1948	**Garden Roller** (later renumbered 381). Unboxed	£5
		Supplied to retailers in trade boxes of 6. Price for a complete box	£50
105b	1948	**Wheelbarrow** (later renumbered 382), brown. Unboxed	£5
		Supplied to retailers in trade boxes of 6. Price for a complete box	£50
105c	1948	**Hand Truck** (later renumbered 383), blue & green versions. Unboxed	£10
		Supplied to retailers in trade boxes of 6. Price for a complete box	£90
105e	1948	**Grass Cutter** (later renumbered 384) red blade version. Unboxed.	£30
		* Add £15 to price guide for green blade version	
		Supplied to retailers in trade boxes of 6. Price for a complete box	£160
107a	1948	**Sack Truck** (later renumbered 385), green. Unboxed	£5
		Supplied to retailers in trade boxes of 6. Price for a complete box	£70
300	1954	**Massey Harris Tractor with metal driver** (formerly 27a), red. Yellow picture box.	£75
		* Add £50 to price guide for later plastic driver versions in colour picture box	
301	1954	**Field Marshall Tractor with metal driver** (formerly 27n), orange. Yellow picture & lift-off lid box versions. * Add £50 to price guide for later plastic driver version	£90
305	1964	**David Brown 990 Tractor.** Colour picture box (unless stated)	
		White with brown engine	£130
		White with brown engine. Bubble pack	£70
		White with red engine	£220
		White with red engine. Bubble pack	£110
		Red/yellow with black engine	£320
		Red/yellow with black engine. Double ended widow box version	£190
308	1971	**Leyland 384 Tractor.** Colour picture box (unless stated)	
		Blue	£80
		Blue in later window box or bubble pack	£40
		Metallic red	£100
		Metallic red in later bubble pack	£50
		Orange	£150
		Orange in later window box or bubble pack	£70
319	1961	**Weeks Tipping Trailer,** red/yellow.	
		Early yellow picture box	£40
		Later window box	£20

343 Dodge Farm Produce Wagon, red cab, blue back & hubs, nr mint in tape repaired box. Sold for £120 DJ Auctions

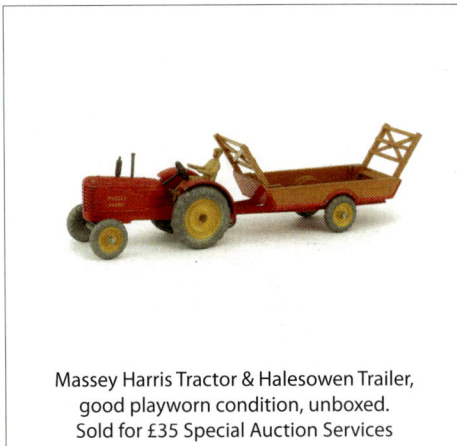

Massey Harris Tractor & Halesowen Trailer, good playworn condition, unboxed. Sold for £35 Special Auction Services

320	1954	**Harvest Trailer** (formerly 27b), metal wheels and plastic hub / rubber tyre versions. Both versions issued with or without front pilot wheel. Yellow box picturing trailer with or without pilot wheel	
		Red trailer, yellow rakes	£30
		Tan trailer, red rakes	£40
321	1954	**Manure Spreader** (formerly 27c), red with metal or plastic shredders. Yellow picture box	£25
322	1954	**Disc Harrow** (formerly 27h). Yellow & colour picture box versions	£15
323	1954	**Triple Gang Mower** (formerly 27j), red. Yellow picture box	£30
324	1954	**Hay Rake** (formely 27k), red. Yellow lift off lid box	£25
340	1954	**Land Rover** (formerly 27d), green, orange & red versions. Yellow picture box.	£80
341	1954	**Land Rover Trailer** (formerly 27m), green, orange & red versions. Yellow picture box	£20
342	1954	**Moto-Cart with metal driver** (formerly 27g), green. Yellow picture box.	£30
343	1954	**Farm Produce Wagon** (formerly 30n), red, green & yellow cab versions. Yellow picture box	£60
344	1970	**Land Rover Pick Up,** blue & red versions. Bubble packed	£35
381	1954	**Garden Roller** (formerly 105a). Unboxed	£5
381	1977	**Convoy Farm Truck,** yellow. Window box	£15
382	1954	**Wheelbarrow** (formerly 105b), brown. Unboxed	£5
383	1954	**Hand Truck** (formerly 105c), blue & green versions.	£10
384	1954	**Grass Cutter** (formerly 105e) red blade version. Unboxed	£35
		* Add £15 to price guide for green blade version	
385	1954	**Sack Truck** (formerly 107a), green. Unboxed	£5
386	1954	**Lawn Mower** (renumbered 751). Yellow lift-off lid box & blue label box versions	£100
563	1948	**Blaw Knox Heavy Tractor with driver** (later renumbered 963), red & orange versions. Early brown & blue picture label box versions.	£45
		Rare dk blue version with mid blue wheels in plain card label box	£320
564	1952	**Elevator Loader** (later renumbered 964), yellow with blue chute.	
		Blue lift-off lid box with orange / white label	£35
		Blue / white strip lift-off lid box	£45
751	1949	**Lawn Mower** (formerly 386). Blue label box	£70

751 Lawnmower, excellent condition in a good blue with orange/white label box

27k Hay Rake, fair condition in early type box. Sold for £35 Special Auction Services

Ref.	First Issued	Model	TPG
963	1954	**Blaw Knox Heavy Tractor** (formerly 563), red & orange versions. Blue/white stripe picture lift off lid box	
		Orange	£45
		Red	£50
		Yellow	£140
964	1960	**Elevator Loader** (formerly 564), blue with yellow chutes. Picture lift-off lid box	£60

GIFT SETS

Ref.	First Issued	Model	TPG
002	1954	**Farmyard Animals 6pce figure set.** Green lift off lid box	£120
006	1954	**Shepherd Set 6pce figure set** (formerly No.6). Green lift off lid box	£120
1	1952	**Farm Vehicles Set;** 27a Massey Harris Tractor, 27b Trailer, 27c Manure Spreader, 27h Harrow, 27k Hay Rake. Blue/white striped box	£520
2	1934	**Farmyard Animals 6pce figure set** (later renumbered 002). Green 'Modelled Miniatures' and 'Dinky Toys' lift off lid box versions.	£120
6	1934	**Shepherd Set 6pce figure set,** HORNBY SERIES on base. Green 'Modelled Miniatures' lift off lid box	£130
6	1936	**Shepherd Set 6pce figure set,** HORNBY SERIES on base. Green 'Dinky Toys' lift off lid box.	£130
6	1946	**Shepherd Set 6pce figure set.** Green 'Modelled Miniatures' lift off lid box	£75
27a	1952	**Tractor & Hay Rake with driver** (later renumbered 310), red. Blue/white striped box	£80
310	1954	**Tractor & Hay Rake** (formerly 27a), red. Yellow lift off lid box	£140
325	1967	**David Brown Tractor & Harrow,** white & red versions. Colour picture box	£110
		* Add £100 to price guide for yellow tractor version	
398	1964	**Farm Equipment Set** (formerly set No.1); 300 Massey Harris Tractor, 320 Trailer, 321 Manure Spreader, 322 Harrow 7 324 Hay Rake. Grey hinged lid box with inner tray	£1,200
399	1969	**Massey Fersuson Tractor & Trailer set,** red. Window box with plain card tray	£160

979 Newmarket Horse Transporter, near mint box complete with correct plastic horses. Sold for £280 Special Auction Services

Rare 28 series MARSH'S SAUSAGE'S van (28k) in mint condition. Sold for £1800 Wallis & Wallis

LORRIES, VANS & COMMERCIALS

14a	1948	**BEV Truck** (renumbered 400), tan or brown driver. Supplied in trade packs of 6 or later in yellow picture box	
		Blue	£20
		Grey	£30
		Complete Trade pack of 6. Sold in 2005	£120
14c	1949	**Coventry Climax Fork Lift,** seated driver, orange/green. Orange lift-off lid picture box, inner card packaging some with test label	
		All orange illustrated box	£30
		Orange box with black illustration and black lettering	£40

22 SERIES

22c	1933	**Motor Truck,** 2pce casting, metal wheels, HORNBY SERIES cast inside. Unboxed	
		Blue cab, red back	£520
		Blue cab, yellow back	£220
		Yellow cab, blue back	£420
22c	1946	**Motor Truck,** 1pce casting, rubber tyres on smooth hubs, open rear window. Unboxed	
		Brown, blue hubs	£100
		Blue	£60
		Red, black hubs	£100
		Mid green, black hubs	£50
		Military green	£480
		Maroon, blue hubs, white tyres	£140
		Turquoise	£70
22d	1933	**Delivery Van,** 2pce casting, HORNBY SERIES or DINKY TOYS cast inside, metal wheels. Unboxed	
		Cream cab, blue back	£8,500
		Orange cab, blue back	£750
		Green cab WE BOYCE livery. Sold in 2008	£17,000
		Black cab, red back MACHESTER GUARDIAN livery. Overpainted in poor condition sold in 2004	£400
		Orange cab, blue back MECCANO ENGINNERING livery. Sold in 2004	£4,500

470 Austin SHELL-BP Van, mint condition
within excellent box.
Sold for £130 Special Auction Services

25m Bedford End Tipper, cream, red hubs,
minor paint touch-ins, unboxed.
Sold for £300 DJ Auctions

25 SERIES LORRIES

Four different versions were produced between 1934-50 with the following casting variations:

> *Type 1 - open chassis without headlights (1934-36)*
> *Type 2 - open chassis with head lights (1936-46)*
> *Type 3 - closed chassis with single open hole (1946-48)*
> *Type 4 - moulded chassis with exhaust (1948-50)*

25a 1934 Open Wagon, with black chassis (unless specified). Unboxed.

Type 1; blue, green, maroon or red versions (black chassis & hubs) £220-250
Type 2; blue, green, maroon or red versions (black chassis & hubs) £150-175
Type 2; blue or green versions (orange chassis). £175-200
Type 2; orange version (green chassis)...£175-200
Type 3; blue, grey, green, orange or stone versions (black chassis & hubs)............................£50-75
Type 3; empty trade box for 6 models. Sold in 2009..£70
Type 4; cream, green, grey, orange or red versions (black chassis & hubs) £40-60
Type 4; mid blue with matching hubs (black chassis). Sold in 2009 ....£170
Type 4; yellow with blue hubs (black chassis).Export colour sold in 2008 ....£220
Type 4; Fawn with black hubs (black chassis). Sold in 2008...£220

25b 1934 Covered Wagon, with black chassis & matching cover (unless specified). Unboxed.

Type 1; blue, cream canopy (black chassis & hubs)
Type 2; cream, green or orange versions with cream canopy (black chassis & hubs) £175-200
Type 2; green CARTER PATTERSON livery...£200
Type 2; orange MECCANO livery £200
Type 2; orange HORNBY TRAINS livery £200
Type 3; blue, grey or green versions, cream canopy (black chassis & hubs)...........................£50-75
Type 4; cream, green, grey, orange or red versions, cream canopy (black chassis, coloured hubs) £50-75
Type 4; fawn with red canopy (black chassis, coloured hubs)..£180
Type 4; yellow with blue canopy (black chassis, coloured hubs).Export colour sold in 2008....£120
SA issue - Type 4; military green (green chassis hubs)...£200

25c 1934 Flat Truck, with black chassis. Unboxed.

Type 1; blue...£150-200
Type 2; green, stone or violet versions £100-150
Type 3; blue, green, grey or stone versions...£50-75
Type 3; stone version sold in 2009..£160
Type 4; blue, fawn, green, orange or yellow versions...£40-50

Scarce variation 25d POOL Petrol Tanker, grey, type 2 open chassis, excellent, unboxed. Sold for £300 DJ Auctions

Scarce variation 25d PETROL Tanker, orange, type 3 clossed chassis, 20 decal to rear, mint unboxed. Sold for £250 DJ Auctions

25d	1934	**Petrol Tank Wagon.** Unboxed.
		Type 1;SHELL BP, CASTROL, REDLINE, ESSO, POWER, PRATTS or TEXACO versions £125-150
		Type1; plain versions £90-110
	1936	Type 2 SHELL BP, CASTROL, REDLINE, ESSO, POWER, POOL or TEXACO versions £100-125
		Type 2; PETROL version £80-100
		Type 3; green, orange or red PETROL versions £100-150
		Type 4; green, orange or red PETROL versions £50-75
25e	1934	**Tipping Wagon,** with black chassis. Unboxed.
		Type 1; maroon cab, yellow back. Sold in 2009 ....£120
		Type 2; brown, fawn, grey or maroon cab versions £50-75
		Type 3; blue, fawn, green or yellow versions £40-60
		Type 4; brown or grey versions £30-50
25f	1934	**Market Gardeners Lorry.** Unboxed.
		Type 1; green or yellow versions...£100-120
		Type 2; grey or yellow versions..£60-80
	1946	Type 3; green, grey or yellow versions £40-60
		Type 4; green, grey, orange or yellow versions £60-80
25g	1935	**Trailer** (later renumbered 429), various colours. Unboxed £15-20
25m	1948	**Bedford Tipper** (renumbered 410). Sold in trade packs of 4 or later in yellow dual numbered picture box
		Dark green cab/back, black, green or red hubs. Unboxed...£90
		Orange cab/back, black or green hubs..£180
		Red cab,cream back, red hubs. Boxed £130
		Yellow cab, light blue back, yellow hubs. Unboxed...£120
		Yellow cab, violet blue back, yellow hubs. Unboxed £240
		Cream cab/back, black or red hubs. Unboxed..£300
		Trade box of 4 red/cream models £520
25r	1948	**Forward Control Lorry** (renumbered 420). Unboxed
		Cream £45
		Green £35
		Grey £80
		Orange..£35
		Trade box of 6. Sold in 2009 ....£180
25s	1937	**6 Wheeled Wagon,** blue, brown, maroon & green versions. Unboxed. £80-90
		* Add £50 to price guide for rare maroon version
25t	1945	**Flat Truck & Trailer** (25c & 25g), orange, blue, green & tan versions. Unboxed...................£90-100

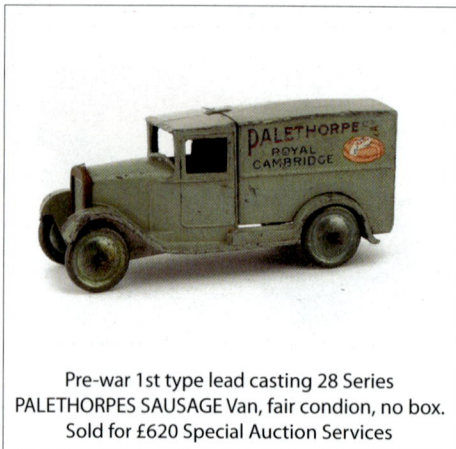

Pre-war 1st type lead casting 28 Series PALETHORPES SAUSAGE Van, fair condion, no box. Sold for £620 Special Auction Services

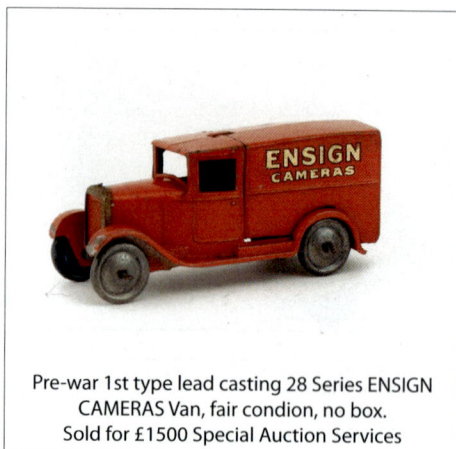

Pre-war 1st type lead casting 28 Series ENSIGN CAMERAS Van, fair condion, no box. Sold for £1500 Special Auction Services

Ref.	First Issued	Model	TPG

25v 1948 **Bedford Refuse Wagon,** tan. Unboxed £30-40
Supplied to retailers in trade boxes of 4. Price for a single model in a trade box £100

25w 1948 **Bedford Truck** (later renumbered 411), lt green cab, body & hubs. Unboxed. £70-80
Supplied to retailers in trade boxes of 4. Price for a single model in a trade box £380

25x 1949 **Commer DINKY SERVICES Breakdown Truck,** grey & tan cab versions. Orange picture box ...£70

28 SERIES DELIVERY VANS

Many of these rarer models seldom come up for sale so we have listed the most recent examples sold, together with their condition which like other early Dinky's are prone to fatigue. All unboxed

Early 2pce body versions

28a	1934	HORNBY TRAINS Delivery Van, orange & yellow versions with coloured wheels. Excellent condition	£2,400
28b	1934	PICKFORDS Delivery Van, blue with white tyres. VG	£1,250
28b	1935	SECCOTINE Delivery Van, blue with white tyres. Fatigue	£340
28c	1934	MANCHESTER GUARDIAN Delivery Van, black/red version, white tyres. Excellent condition	£1,000
28d	1934	OXO Delivery Van, blue. No fatigue paint loss only	£1,400
28e	1934	ENSIGN CAMERAS Delivery Van, blue. Excellent condition (2003)	£4,100
28e	1934	FIRESTONE TYRES Delivery Van, white. Excellent condition	£850
28h	1934	SHARPS TOFFEE Delivery Van, black/red. Excellent condition	£2,200
28h	1935	DUNLOP Delivery Van, red with white tyres. Fatigue & retouched	£120
28k	1934	MARSH's SAUSAGES Delivery Van, green. Excellent condition	£1,900
28l	1934	CRAWFORDS Delivery Van, red. Repaint	£160
28m	1934	CASTROL Delivery Van, green. VG	£3,800
28n	1934	MECCANO Delivery Van, yellow. Excellent condition	£5,600
28n	1935	ATCO Delivery Van, green. Excellent condition	£850
28p	1935	CRAWFORDS Delivery Van, red, later 1pce diecast body version. Excellent condition	£4,800

Later 1pce body versions

28a	1936	GOLDEN SHRED Delivery Van, cream with white tyres. Fatigue crazing & repair	£220
28d	1935	OXO, blue. Slight fatigue	£150
28f	1934	PALETHORPES Delivery Van, pale blue. Minor fatigue	£110
28f	1938	VIROL Delivery Van, blue. VG condition with slight restoration	£380
28g	1934	KODAK Delivery Van, yellow. Fatigue	£80
28h	1935	DUNLOP Delivery Van, red with white tyres. Fatigue & retouched	£120
28r	1936	SWAN PENS Delivery Van, black. Unboxed no fatigue. Modified restoration 3cm longer than standard 28 series vans	£40

Pre-war 1st type lead casting 28 Series
KODAK Van, fair condion, no box.
Sold for £1500 Special Auction Services

Pre-war 1st type lead casting 28 Series
PICKFORDS Van, fair condion, no box.
Est. £500+ unsold Special Auction Services

28s	1936	**FRYS Delivery Van,** brown & cream versions. Excellent condition	£660
28t	1936	**OVALTINE Delivery Van,** red with white tyres. Minor fatigue	£300
28w	1936	**OSRAM Delivery Van,** yellow with white tyres. Minor fatigue	£200
28x	1936	**HOVIS Delivery Van,** white with white tyres. VG	£200
28y	1936	**EXIDE Delivery Van,** red. VG	£260
28	-	**SA issue:** Military green version	£380

280 SERIES DELIVERY VANS

280	1945	**Delivery Van** (without advertising), red & blue versions. Unboxed.	£40-50
		* Military green model sold for £480 (2006)	
		Supplied to retailers in trade boxes of . Price for complete box of 6 models	£460
280a	1937	**VIYELLA Delivery Van,** blue with white tyres. Unboxed, covered in varnish	£160
280b	1937	**LYONS TEA Delivery Van,** blue. Unboxed in excellent condition	£240
280b	1939	**HARTLEYS JAM Delivery Van,** cream with white tyres. Unboxed in excellent condition with no fatigue	£380
280c	1937	**SHREDDED WHEAT Delivery Van,** cream, red stripe with white tyres. Unboxed in excellent condition with no fatigue	£900
280d	1937	**BISTO Delivery Van,** yellow with white tyres. Unboxed. Unboxed with fatigue crazing	£90
280e	1937	**ECKO Delivery Van,** green. Unboxed with slight fatigue (2005)	£260
280f	1938	**YORKSHIRE EVENING POST Delivery Van,** cream with white tyres. Unboxed no fatigue	£170
280f	1937	**MACKINTOSHS Delivery Van,** red with white tyres. Unboxed no fatigue	£190

Pre-war 1st type lead casting 28 Series OXO
Van, fair condion, no box.
Est. £500+ unsold Special Auction Services

Pre-war empty yellow box for 28 Series Vans,
fair condition lacking dividers.
Sold for £800 Special Auction Services

Ref.	First Issued	Model	TPG

RARE 'EXCLUSIVE' PROMOTIONALS

280g	1939	**BENTALLS Delivery Van,** green/yellow. Unboxed	£7,500
280h	1939	**MAISON DE BONNETERIE Delivery Van,** red. Unboxed. Only 1 example known	£2,500
280j	1939	**FENWICK Delivery Van,** green. Unboxed	£7,500
280k	1939	**HG LOOSE Delivery Van,** green. Unboxed. * Only 2 examples of this model known	£8,500

30 SERIES TRUCKS

30e	1935	**Breakdown Crane,** brown, grey, light blue, red, green & yellow versions. Unboxed.	
		1st type; Mazac wheels, open rear window	£200-250
		2nd type, rubber tyres, flat hubs, open rear window	£100-150
		3rd type; rubber tyres, ridged hubs, no rear window	£30-50
		3rd type; scarce green version	£100
30j	1950	**Austin Wagon** (later renumbered 412), blue & maroon versions. Unboxed	£90-100
		Supplied to retailers in trade boxes of 6. Price for 1 model with trade box	£180
		Brown version. Sold in 2008	£240
		Red version. Sold in 2008	£160
30m	1950	**Rear Tipping Wagon** (later renumbered 414), dk red & orange versions. Unboxed	£60-70
		* £50-60 price guide for blue version	
30n	1950	**Farm Produce Wagon** (later renumbered 343), green, red & yellow cab versions. Unboxed	£50-60
30p	1950	**Petrol Tanker,** MOBILGAS or PETROL lettering on tank, green & red versions. Yellow	
		dual numbered picture box	£110-120
30p	1952	**Petrol Tanker** (renumbered 441), CASTROL lettering on tank, green. Yellow picture box	£70-80
30p	1952	**Petrol Tanker** (later renumbered 441), ESSO lettering on tank, red Yellow picture box	£70-80
30r	1951	**Fordson Thames Flat Truck** (later renumbered 422), green & red versions. Unboxed.	£50-60
		* Brown version sold for £190	
30s	1950	**Austin Covered Wagon** (renumbered 413), maroon, mid blue & green versions. U/b.	£120-130
		* Dk blue cab version sold for £170	
30v	1949	**EXPRESS DAIRY Electric Dairy Van** (renumbered 490), grey & cream versions. U/b	£60
		Supplied to retailers in trade boxes of 6. Price for 6 boxed models	£440
30v	1949	**NCB Electric Dairy Van** (later renumbered 491), grey & cream versions. Unboxed	£60
30w	1952	**Hindle Smart Helecs BRITISH RAILWAYS** (later renumbered 421), dk red. Unboxed	£45

969 BBC TV Extending Mast Vehicle, dark green, lt grey flash complete with mast & dish, excellent in a VG box. Sold for £100 Wallis & Wallis

33r CARTER PATTERSON Mechanical Horse & Trailer, dk green, VG condition. Sold for £140 Wallis & Wallis

31 SERIES VANS

31a	1951	ESSO Trojan 15cwt Van (later renumbered 450), red. Unboxed	£60
31b	1952	DUNLOP Trojan 15cwt Van (later renumbered 451), red. Unboxed	£60
31c	1951	CHIVERS Trojan 15cwt Van (later renumbered 452), green. Unboxed	£60
31d	1953	OXO Trojan 15cwt Van (later renumbered 453), blue. Unboxed	£150

33 SERIES

Prices relate to unboxed cabs & trailers sold during the past 2 years.

33a & 33b	1935	Mechanical Horse & Flat Truck Trailer, non advertising version in various colours. Unboxed	£60-80
33a & 33d	1935	Mechanical Horse & HORNBY TRAINS Box Van Trailer	£600
33a & 33d	1935	Mechanical Horse & MECCANO Box Van Trailer	£200
33a & 33e	1935	Mechanical Horse & Dust Cart Trailer	£150
33a & 33f	1935	Mechanical Horse & CASTROL Petrol Tanker	£140
33a & 33f	1935	Mechanical Horse & ESSO Petrol Tanker	£125
33a & 33f	1935	Mechanical Horse & (non advertising) Petrol Tanker	£110
33a & 33r	1935	Mechanical Horse & SOUTHERN RAILWAYS Trailer	£320
33a & 33r	1935	Mechanical Horse & LMS RAILWAYS Trailer	£160
33a & 33r	1935	Mechanical Horse & GWR RAILWAYS Trailer	£125
33a & 33r	1935	Mechanical Horse & LNER RAILWAYS Trailer	£130
33w	1934	Mechanical Horse & Wagon, green, grey, brown, red, yellow & cream versions. Unboxed	£70-80

34b Royal Mail Van, later example with filled in rear windows, red, black bonnet, minor chipping, unboxed. Sold for £80 Wallis & Wallis

34C Trade box containing 6 blue Loudspeaker Vans, excellent in a VG box. Sold for £160 Toy Price Guide Archive

Ref.	First Issued	Model		TPG

34 SERIES

34a	1935	**ROYAL AIR MAIL SERVICE Vehicle,** blue. Unboxed	£160
34b	1938	**ROYAL MAIL Van,** red. Unboxed.	
		red, black roof & nose version	£40
		red version with black nose only	£120
34c	1948	**Loudspeaker Van,** silver or black roof speakers. Unboxed	
		Blue	£35
		Brown	£150
		Fawn	£60
		Green	£80
60y	1938	**Thompson Aircraft Tender,** driver cast-in, red. Unboxed	£150
151b	1937	**6 Wheel Covered Wagon** (later renumbered 25s), green. Unboxed	£50
252	1954	**Bedford Refuse Wagon,** lime green & beige versions. Yellow picture box	£50-60
		* Add £150 to price guide for orange cab versions	
260	1955	**ROYAL MAIL Morris Van,** red. Yellow picture box	£60-70
261	1955	**Morris TELEPHONE SERVICES Van,** green/black. Yellow picture box	£70
273	1965	**Mini Minor RAC Van,** blue, white roof. Yellow/red picture box containing inner packing ring	£70
274	1964	**Mini Minor AA Van,** yellow, white roof, pre 60s logo.	
	1964	Yellow/red picture box version	£60
	1967	Colour picture box version	£80
	1969	JOSEPH MASON PAINTS Mini Minor Van, dk red with PAINTS roof sign. Promotional model in red box with protective inner card ring	£1,500
275	1964	**Brinks Armoured Car,** 2 figures & 2 crates, grey/blue. Window box	£20
		US issue SECURITY SERVICE 1859, thought to be sales representatives model, in rare Brinks presentation box. Sold in 2003	£420
		Unboxed Mexican issue, dark grey body & roof without driver	£190
280	1966	**MIDLAND BANK Mobile Lorry plastic figure,** white/silver. Colour picture box with inner card ring	£80-90
381	1977	**Farm Truck.** Window box	£10-15
383	1978	**NCL Truck.** Window box	£15-20

989 U.S. export AUTO TRANSPORTERS Car Carrier, yellow cab, grey back, lt blue ramps, excellent unboxed. Sold for £560 Wallis & Wallis

410 Beford End Tipper, yellow cab & hubs, blue back, mint in excellent box. Sold for £210 DJ Auctions

385	1977	**ROYAL MAIL Truck.** Window box	£15-20
400	1954	**BEV Truck (formerly 14a),** standing metal driver, blue & grey versions. Yellow picture box	£25-30
401	1954	**Coventry Climax Fork Lift,** driver,	
	-	Orange, yellow lift off lid box with metal driver	£30-40
	-	Orange, yellow lift off lid box with blue plastic driver	£280
	-	Orange, blue/white stripe lift off lid box with metal driver	£30-40
	-	Red, blue/white stripe lift off lid box with metal driver	£540
402	1966	**COCA COLA Bedford Truck,** red with white roof, 6 bottle crates. Colour picture box	£110-120
404	1967	**Climax Fork Lift,** red/yellow & yellow versions. Colour picture box	£35
407	1966	**KENWOOD Ford Transit Van,** blue & white versions. Colour picture box	£60
407	1970	**HERTZ Ford Transit Van,** yellow. Colour picture box & bubble pack versions	£50
407	1970	**PELTZ BADKEREI Ford Transit Van,** blue/yellow. Colour picture box	£80-100
408	1956	**Big Bedford Lorry** (later renumbered 522 & 922), blue & dk red versions. Yellow & blue/white stripe lift-off lid versions	£150-175
		Pink cab version, unboxed. Sold in 2004	£800
409	1956	**Bedford Articulated Lorry** (later renumbered 521 & 921), glazed & unglazed window versions. Yellow lift-off lid box	£100-120
410	1954	**Bedford End Tipper** (formerly 25m), cream, red, red/cream & yellow/blue versions. Within 1st type yellow picture box	£80-100
		Within later yellow/red card box	£110-130
410	1972	**ROYAL MAIL Bedford CF Van,** red, Speedwheels. Window box	£15
		20cm x 15cm window poster for above model. Sold in 2006	£30
410	1974	**JOHN MENZIES Bedford CF Van,** blue, Speedwheels. Window box	£15
410	1974	**BELACO Bedford CF Van,** brown/black, Speedwheels. Window box	£40-50
410	1975	**MJ HIRE CF Bedford Van,** white, Speedwheels. Window box	£15
410	1975	**MARLEY TILES CF Bedford Van,** red, Speedwheels. Window box	£15
410	1975	**DANISH POST Bedford CF Van,** yellow, Speedwheels. Window box	£40-50
410	1975	**SIMPSONS Bedford CF Van,** red/black, Speedwheels. Window box	£15
		* We have only included the models produced by Dinky, several Code 2 versions exist to which we attach a £15 price guide	
411	1954	**Bedford Truck** (formerly 25w), green. Yellow picture box	£70-80
412	1954	**Austin Wagon** (formerly 30j), dk red & dk blue versions. Unboxed	£40-50
		Generally supplied to retailers in trade boxes of 6. Price for a single model in a trade box	£100
		Yellow unboxed version	£140
		Lt blue unboxed version	£120
		For later models in yellow picture box	£70-80

Scarce 502 Foden Type1 Flat Truck, dk blue, red flash, red back & hubs, no hook, excellent in VG brown box. Sold for £1400 DJ Auctions

422 Fordson Thames Flat Truck, red, mint in mint box. Sold for £120 DJ Auctions

Ref.	First Issued	Model	TPG
412	1974	**Bedford CF AA Van,** yellow with roof sign. Window box	£25-30
413	1954	**Austin Covered Wagon** (formerly 30s), various red & blue versions. Yellow picture box	£120-150
414	1954	**Dodge Rear Tipping Wagon** (formerly 30m), green, orange, red, grey & blue versions. Yellow picture box	£90-110
415	1954	**Mechanical Horse & Wagon** (formerly 33w), blue & red versions. Yellow picture box	£90-110
416	1975	**Ford MOTORWAY SERVICES Transit Van with cones & signs,** yellow. Window box	£40-50
417	1956	**Leyland Comet Lorry** (later renumbered 931). Yellow lift-off lid box.	
		Dark blue cab, brown back, red hubs. Scarce version sold in 2006	£320
		Violet blue cab, yellow back, red hubs	£100
	-	Yellow cab, green back & hubs	£200
418	1956	**Leyland Comet Lorry with Tailboard** (later renumbered 932) blue & green versions. Blue/white stripe & yellow lift-off lid box	
		Dark blue cab, mid blue back, cream hubs	£200
		Green cab, orange back, green hubs	£170
		Green cab, orange back, cream hubs	£200
420	1954	**Forward Control Lorry** (formerly 25r), red, green & blue versions. Yellow picture box	£70-90
421	1955	**BRITISH RAILWAYS Hindle Smart Helecs** (formerly30w) dk red. Yellow picture box	£100
422	1954	**Fordson Thames Flat Truck** (formerly 30r), red & green versions. Yellow picture box	£90-110
424	1963	**Commer Articulated Truck,** yellow/grey with interchangeable plastic stake body & blue plastic canopy. Plain presentation box with inner display tray	£110
425	1964	**Bedford TK HALL & CO Coal Wagon,** 6 coal bags & scales, red. Colour lift-off lid picture box	£110
428	1956	**Large Trailer** (later renumbered 951), grey, red & yellow versions. Yellow picture box	£25
429	1954	**Trailer** (formerly 25g), red & green versions. Yellow picture box	£25
430	1954	**Commer DINKY SERVICES Breakdown Truck with crane, tan cab.**	
		* Add £100 to price guide for cream or red boxed versions	
		Early version without windows, yellow lift-off lid box	£120
		Later version with windows, yellow lift-off lid box	£160
		Glazed window version, blue/white stripe box	£100
430	1977	**Johnson 2 Ton Dumper,** 2-tone orange versions. Window box	£20

503 Foden Type 1 Flat Truck with Tailboard, lt grey, blue flash, red hubs, minor paint touch-ins in excellent brown box. Sold for £1000 DJ Auctions

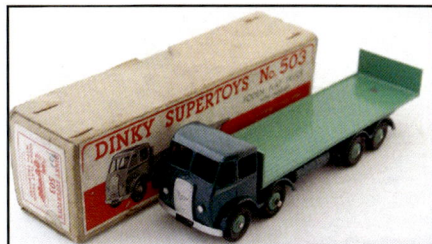

503 Foden Type 1 Flat Truck with Tailboard, dk green cab, lt green flash, back & hubs, no hook, mint in excellent brown box. Sold for £960 DJ Auctions

GUY TRUCKS

Identification Guidelines:
First released in 1947, numbered 511-514, two slight cab casting changes were made to the number plate bracket as follows:

> *1st type cab; 1947-54 no bracket to either side of the number plate.*
> *1st type packaging; Blue, green or plain brown lift-off lid boxes with either orange/white or red/white lid labels*
> *2nd type cab; 1954-58 bracket either side of number plate*
> *2nd type packaging; Blue/white striped lift-off lid boxes*

In 1954 Guy Trucks were re-numbered 911-913. These all came with 2nd type cab casting and were packaged in blue/white stripe lift-off lid boxes

In 1956 there was a final re-numbering to 431-433, again all issued in the 2nd type cab casting but packaged in yellow lift-off lid illustrated boxes. To add confusion Guy Warriors (rounded cabs) were introduced in 1958 using the same numbering. These came in all yellow illustrated card boxes.

431	1956	**Guy 4 Ton Truck.** Yellow lift-off lid box
		All light blue cab, chassis, back & hub version. Sold in 2008...£560
		Red cab, chassis & hubs. Fawn back...£640
		Violet blue cab & chassis. Mid blue back & hubs £170
431	1958	**Guy Warrior 4 Ton lorry** (rounded cab). Yellow illustrated all card box
		Red cab, green back with windows £2,600
		Tan cab, green back with windows..£200
		Tan cab, green back without windows £280
432	1956	**Guy Flat Truck.** Yellow lift-off lid box
		Mid blue cab, chassis & hubs. Red back...£120
		Red cab & chassis. Mid blue back & hubs. Sold in 2009 ....£1,000
		Violet blue cab & chassis. Red back. Mid blue hubs £120
432	1958	**Guy Warrior Flat Truck** (rounded cab), green cab, red back. Yellow illustrated all card box
		With windows...£280
		Without windows £160
433	1956	**Guy Flat Truck with Tailboard.** Yellow lift-off lid box
		Dark green (1st type) cab & chassis. Mid green back & hubs £180
		Light blue cab, chassis & hubs. Orange back £800
		Violet blue cab & chassis. Orange back. Mid blue hubs £190
432	1976	**Foden Tipping Lorry,** white cab. Window box..£25
434	1964	**Bedford TK Crash Truck,** white with TOP RANK decal. Colour picture box...........................£80
		* Add £30 to price guide for red AUTO SERVICES version
435	1964	**Bedford TK Tipper,** white, grey, red & blue cab versions. Yellow/red picture box £110
		* Add £100 to price guide for yellow version

443 Studebaker NATIONALE BENZOLE Tanker,
yellow, mint in excellent box.
Sold for £235 DJ Auctions

501 Foden Type1 Diesel 8 Wheel Wagon, dk
blue, silver flash, no hook, dk blue hubs, mint in
excellent brown box. Sold for £850 DJ Auctions

Ref.	First Issued	Model	TPG
436	1963	**ATLAS COPCO Truck,** yellow. Yellow picture box	£110
438	1970	**Ford D800 Tipper Truck,** red. Colour picture box & bubble pack versions	£40-60
		* Add £30 to price guide for orange version	
		POLYCARB promotional, white box.	£150
		Heavy Transport EEC Ltd promotional, colour picture box	£100
439	1970	**Ford D800 Snow Plow,** various blue & orange cab versions all with yellow plough. Colour picture box	£70
		* Add £30 to price guide for red plough version	
440	1977	**Ford D800 Tipper Truck,** orange & red cab versions. Window box	£20
440	1954	**MOBILGAS Petrol Tanker** (formerly 30p), red. Yellow picture box.	£80
441	1954	**CASTROL Petrol Tanker** (formerly 30p), green. Yellow picture box	£80
442	1973	**Land Rover Breakdown Crane,** white/red. Bubble pack	£40-50
442	1954	**ESSO Petrol Tanker** (formerly 30p), red. Yellow picture box	£80
443	1957	**NATIONAL Petrol Tanker,** yellow. Yellow picture box	£100
448	1963	**Cheverolet El Camino Pick-Up with Trailers,** lt blue with ACME HIRE livery. Yellow lift off lid box with internal packaging	£240
449	1961	**Cheverolet El Camino Pick-Up,** 2-tone white/lt blue version. Yellow picture box	£130
449	1977	**Johnston Road Sweeper** (formerly 451), non opening doors, black plastic pipes & brush. Window box	
		Lime green cab & back	£30
		Orange cab, metallic green back	£25
		Yellow VACU-SWEEP. Promotional issue for ILLINOIS CLEANING CO.	£60
		Blue cab, white back JUMBO CLEANING CO. Pre-production issue sold in 2007	£180
450	1954	**ESSO Trojan Van** (formerly 31a), red. Yellow picture box	£150
450	1965	**Bedford CASTROL TK Truck,** green. Picture lift-off lid box	£110
451	1954	**DUNLOP Trojan Van** (formerly 31b), red. Yellow picture box	£150
451	1971	**Johnston Road Sweeper** (renumbered 449), opening doors, black plastic pipes & brush	
		Orange cab, metallic green back. Pictorial box or bubble pack versions	£45
		Lime green cab & back. Bubble pack	£80
		Yellow cab & back, with or without JOHNSTON decal. Pictorial box or bubble pack (made exclusively for the Johnston Company)	£120

465 Morris J CAPSTAN van, 2-tone blue, mint in excellent box. Sold for £160 DJ Auctions

482 Bedford DINKY TOYS 10 CWT Van, 2-tone yellow, mint in mint box. Sold for £220 DJ Auctions

452	1954	**CHIVERS Trojan Van** (formerly 31c), green. Yellow picture box..£130
453	1954	**OXO Trojan Van,** blue. Unboxed..£150
454	1957	**CYDRAX Trojan Van,** lt green. Yellow picture box £140
455	1957	**BROOKE BOND Trojan Van,** red, ridged hubs. Yellow picture box. ....£140 Promotional issue: Labels to van roof and box bearing 'Little Red Vans' legend. Sold in 2002 £380
465	1959	**CAPSTAN Morris 10cwt Van,** blue. Yellow picture box...£180
470	1954	**Austin A40 SHELL-BP Van,** red / green version with decals. Yellow picture box £90
470	1954	**Austin A40 OMNISPORT Van,** lt blue with red 'Omnisport Todo Para El Deporte livery. Unboxed ....£6,400 *This model was first seen and sold by Wallis & Wallis in 2009, believed to be a 1957 South American promotional (possibly El Salvador).*
471	1955	**Austin A40 NESTLES Van,** red. Yellow picture box £100
472	1956	**Austin A40 RALEIGH Van,** green. Yellow picture box £100
480	1954	**Bedford CA KODAK Van,** yellow. Yellow picture box..£80
481	1955	**Bedford CA OVALTINE Van,** blue. Yellow picture box £100
482	1956	**Bedford DINKY TOYS Van,** orange / yellow. Yellow picture box..£120
490	1954	**EXPRESS DAIRIES Electric Van,** grey & cream versions. Yellow picture box...........................£70
491	1954	**NCB Electric Van,** grey & cream versions. Yellow box £130
492	1954	**Loudspeaker Van** (formerly 34c, 280 series casting), blue with black or silver roof speakers. Yellow picture box £50
492	1964	**Election Mini Van,** orange roof speakers with plastic figure, microphone & cable, white, 'Vote for Somebody' decal. Window box £125

501 Foden Type1 Diesel 8 Wheel Wagon, red cab, silver flash, fawn back, no hook, red hubs, nr mint in good brown box. Sold for £340 DJ Auctions

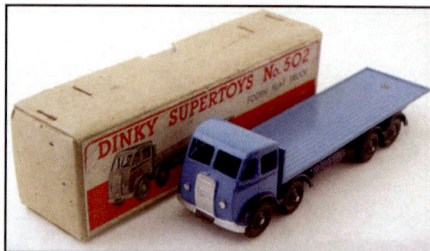

Scarce 502 Foden Type1 Flat Truck, mid blue, dk blue flash, no hook, blue hubs, mint in excellent brown box. Sold for £1500 DJ Auctions

500 SERIES FODEN TRUCKS

From their 1947 release the 500 series Fodens were issued in 2 distinctive cab styles prior to being renumbered as the 900 series in 1954 as follows:

    1st type; 1947-52 rectangular radiator grill with FODEN lettering

    2nd type; 1952-64 with wider 'gull wing' radiator grill style and without FODEN lettering.

From 1947-54 the 500 series Fodens came in 3 variations of lift-off lid boxes as follows:

    blue box with orange/white label

    plain brown card box with red/white label

    green box with red/white label

*Look out for rare US issues identied by a unique HUDSON DOBSON labels to one side of the box

Warning! Highly prized by Dinky collectors, Fodens have been the subject of much repainting and we recommend that when purchasing models collectors thoroughly check baseplates, axles and hubs ensuring condition for each is the same and don't arouse suspision as several models and unusual variations have turned up at provincial auctions produced by highly skilled professional paintshops and passed of as rare or unusual colour variations.

Prices below are for mint boxed models

501	1947	**Foden 8 Wheel Wagon** (1st type), tow hook on some models.	
		Red cab, fawn back, red hubs, brown hubs	£170
		Brown cab, brown back, brown hubs	£200
		All grey issue with red cab flash & red hubs (no hook)	£540
		Dk blue cab with silver flash, mid blue back, blue hubs	£130
		Dk blue cab, mid blue back, blue hubs (no hook)	£600
		US issue: Red cab with silver flash & red hubs (no hook). HUDSON DOBSON box label	£420
501	1952	**Foden 8 Wheel Wagon** (2nd type). Later renumbered 901	
		Violet cab, mid blue back, blue hubs	£800
		Dk red cab, fawn back, red hubs	£1,300
502	1947	**Foden 8 Flat Truck** (1st type).	
		Dk green cab, mid green back, green hubs	£240
		Dk green cab, mid green back, green hubs	£1,000
		Mid blue cab, mid blue back, blue hubs	£750
		Dk blue cab, red back, blue hubs	£170
		Orange cab, mid green back, green hubs	£300
502	1952	**Foden 8 Flat Truck** (2nd type). Later renumbered 902	
		Orange cab, mid green back, green hubs	£240
		Blue cab, red back, blue hubs	£2,200
		Yellow cab, green back, green hubs	£540

502 Foden Type1 Flat Truck, green, silver flash, no hook, green hubs, nr mint in a torn brown box. Sold for £400 DJ Auctions

504 Foden Type 1 14 Ton Tanker, violet blue cab, silver flash, lt blue tank & hubs, mint in excellent brown box. Sold for £560 DJ Auctions

503	1947	**Foden 8 Flat Truck with Tailboard** (1st type) £750-900
		Red cab, red back, red hubs £240
		Dk green cab, mid green back, green hubs £120
		Dk green cab, mid green back, green hubs £2,100
		Grey cab, grey back, blue hubs £2,300
		Violet cab, orange back, blue hubs £1,400
503	1952	**Foden 8 Flat Truck with Tailboard** (2nd type). Later renumbered 903
		Dk green cab, mid green back, green hubs £4,400
		Orange cab, yellow back, yellow hubs £4,000
		Dk blue cab, yellow back, blue hubs £750
		Violet cab, orange back, blue hubs £600
504	1948	**Foden Tanker** (1st type)
		Dk blue cab, lt blue tanker £100
		Red cab, fawn tanker £280
504	1952	**Foden Tanker** (2nd type), red cab & tank. £140-180
	1953	MOBILGAS logo to sides and tank end £200
	1953	MOBILGAS logo to sides and PEGASUS decal to tank end only. Sold in 2009 ....£1,200
505	1952	**Foden 8 Flat Truck & Chains** (1st type).
		All maroon with silver cab flash. Sold in 2009 ....£2,200
		All green cab with lt. Green cab flash. Sold in 2009 ....£1,500
505	1954	**Foden 8 Flat Truck & Chains** (2nd type). Later renumbered 905
		All maroon £320
		All green £190

502 Foden Type1 Flat Truck, orange cab, green flash & hubs, fawn back, no hook, excellent in blue export label box. Sold for £800 DJ Auctions

503 Foden Type 1 Flat Truck with Tailboard, red, black flash, red hubs, mint in excellent brown box. Sold for £1500 DJ Auctions

500 SERIES GUY TRUCKS

See models numbers 431-433 for more information. Prices below are for mint boxed models:

511	1947	**Guy 4 Ton Lorry** (1st type).	
		Brown cab, back & hubs. Black chassis	£190
		Fawn cab, back, red chassis & hubs	£340
		Green cab, back & hubs. Black chassis	£260
		Red cab, chassis & hubs. Fawn back	£90
		Violet blue cab & chassis. Mid blue back & hubs	£150
511	1954	**Guy 4 Ton Lorry** (2nd type)	
		Mid blue cab, back, chassis & hubs	£340
		Violet blue cab & chassis. Mid blue back & hubs	£260
512	1947	**Guy Flat Truck** (1st type)	
		Dark Blue cab, chassis. Red back. Mid blue hubs	£150
		Brown cab & chassis. Green back & hubs	£300
		Dark green cab & chassis. Light green back & hubs	£950
		Fawn cab & back. Red chassis & hubs	£1,900
		Khaki green cab, back & hubs. Black chassis	£260
		Maroon cab, back & hubs. Black chassis	£260
		Orange cab & chassis. Green back & hubs	£500
		Teal blue cab & chassis. Red back. mid blue hubs	£560
		Yellow cab & back. Red hubs. Black Chassis	£300
512	1954	**Guy Flat Truck** (2nd type)	
		Red cab & chassis. Blue back & hubs	£900
		Mid blue cab, chassis & hubs. Red back	£150
		Red cab, back & chassis. Blue hubs	£170
		Violet blue cab & chassis. Red back. Mid blue hubs	£400
513	1947	**Guy Flat Truck & Tailboard** (1st type)	£225-275
		Green cab & back. Black chassis & hubs	
		Dark green cab & chassis. Light green back & hubs	£130
		Grey cab & back. Black chassis & hubs	£220
		Yellow cab & back. Black chassis & hubs	£130
		Yellow cab & back. Navy chassis & hubs	£140
		Violet blue cab & chassis. Orange back. Mid blue hubs.	£150
		Violet blue cab & chassis. Orange back. Mid blue hubs.US HUDSON DOBSON box label packaging	£200
513	1954	**Guy Flat Truck & Tailboard** (2nd type)	
		Violet blue cab & chassis. Red back. Mid blue hubs	£200

Rare 522 Big Bedford Lorry, cerise, cream back & hubs, VG re-touched, unboxed. Sold for £150 Wallis & Wallis

514 Guy WEETABIX Van, yellow, mint in excellent blue box. Sold for £2500 DJ Auctions

Ref.	First Issued	Model	TPG
514	1950	**Guy Van SLUMBERLAND** (1st type), red. Blue lift off lid bix with, orange/white label	
		Red 'ridged' hub version	£500
		Red 'recessed' hub version	£800
		Black hub version	£1,700
514	1952	**Guy Van LYONS** (1st type), dk blue, mid blue ridged hubs. Blue lift off lid bix with,	
		orange/white label	£800
514	1952	**Guy Van WEETABIX** (1st type), yellow. Blue lift off lid bix with, orange/white label	
		Yellow 'ridged' hub version	£600
		Yellow 'recessed' hub version	£1,500
514	1953	**Guy Van SPRATTS** (1st type), red/cream with red recessed hubs. Blue lift off lid bix with,	
		orange/white label	£360
521	1948	**Bedford Articulated Lorry,** yellow or red versions. Brown or blue label box	£70
522	1952	**Big Bedford Lorry** (later renumbered 922), blue & dk red versions. Blue label box....................	£90
531	1949	**Leyland Comet Lorry with Stake Board** (later renumbered 931), yellow & red cab versions.	
		Blue label box	£140
		* Increase price guide by £150 for blue cab version	
532	1952	**Leyland Comet Lorry with Hinged Tailboard** (later renumbered 932), green & blue cab	
		versions. Blue label box.	£140
533	1953	**Leyland Comet Cement Wagon,** yellow with FERROCRETE & PORTLAND BLUE CIRCLE	
		CEMENT decals.	
		Blue lift-off lid box with orange/white label	£150
		Blue/white striped box with inner card protector	£170
551	1948	**Trailer** (later renumbered 991), grey version.	£10-15
		* Add £40 to price guide for yellow & green versions	
		Supplied to retailers in trade boxes of 3. Price for a complete trade box	£90
563	1948	**Blaw Know Heavy Tractor** (later renumbered 963), red & orange versions. Brown or blue	
		label box.	£50
		* Add £250 to price guide for rare dk blue version..	£50
571	1949	**Coles Mobile Crane** (later renumbered 971), yellow/black. Blue label box.................................	£60
581	1953	**BRITISH RAILWAYS Horsebox**, maroon. Brown or blue box with orange/white label..........	£110
		EXPRESS HORSE VAN HIRE SERVICE livery, US export issue	£1,400

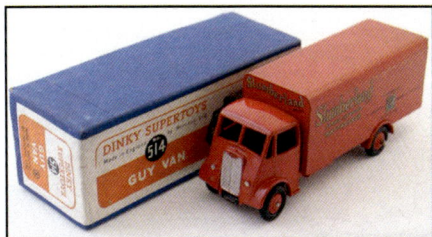

514 Guy SLUMBERLAND Van, red, mint in mint blue box. Sold for £560 DJ Auctions

514 Guy LYONS SWISS ROLLS Van, blue, minor paint touch-ins in excellent blue box. Sold for £1200 DJ Auctions

582	1953	**Pullmore Car Transporter** (later renumbered 982), trailer with 4 rivets (rarer issues have 6). Blue/white striped box with inner packing card	
		Light blue cab, trailer (4 rivets) & hubs, fawn decks	£120
		Light blue cab, trailer (6 rivet version) & hubs, fawn decks	£160
		Mid blue cab, light blue trailer (4 rivets), hubs & decks	£110
		Mid blue cab, trailer (4 rivets) & hubs, fawn decks. Plain blue box with end labels	£1,100
591	1952	**AEC SHELL Tanker** (later renumbered 991), red/yellow. Blue label & blue/white stripe box versions	£120
752	1953	**Goods Yard Crane** (later renumbered 973), yellow with blue base. Blue label & blue/white stripe box	£60
887		Pre-production Unic Tanker, black cab. Intended as a Dutch promotional for NEDERLANSCHE WEG MAATCHAPPY (Dutch Road Building Co.)	£900

930 Bedford Pallet Jekta Van includes the
3 pallets, chipped, pen maks to box.
Sold for £160 Wallis & Wallis

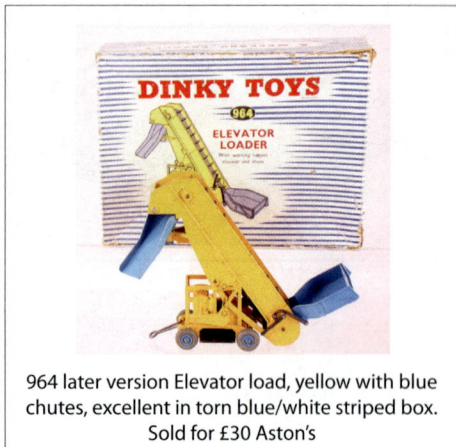

964 later version Elevator load, yellow with blue
chutes, excellent in torn blue/white striped box.
Sold for £30 Aston's

900 SERIES FODEN TRUCKS

Introduced in 1954 all 900 series Fodens were issued with 2nd type cabs with the 'gull wing radiator style without FODEN lettering and packaged in the later style blue/white striped boxes, with early issues in dual numbered boxes to use up stock during the cross over period.

Prices below are for mint models in single blue/white stripe single numbered boxes unless specified.

901	1954	**Foden 8 Wheel Wagon** (formerly 501).
		Red cab, fawn back, red hubs. £280
		Violet cab, fawn back, blue hubs. £620
		Dk green cab, mid green back, green hubs. £200
902	1954	**Foden Flat Truck** (formerly 502)
		Dark Blue cab, red back, mid blue hubs. Sold in 2006 ....£480
		Yellow cab, mid green back, green hubs. £700
		Orange cab, mid green rear, green hubs..£300
		Red cab, mid green rear, green hubs...£750
903	1954	**Foden Flat Truck with Tailboard** (formerly 503)
		Mid blue cab, lt brown rear, blue hubs..£340
		Violet blue cab, orange rear, blue hubs. £280
		Violet blue cab, yellow rear, blue hubs. £800
		Yellow cab, yellow rear, green hubs...£680
		Yellow cab, yellow rear, green hubs. Rare dual numbered blue/white striped box £1,200
		Orange cab, orange rear, green hubs. £900
905	1954	**Foden Flat Truck with Chains** (formerly 505)
		Red cab, grey rear, red hubs...£180
		Maroon cab, maroon rear, red hubs. £180
		Green cab, green rear, green hubs. £220
		Mid blue cab, grey rear, blue hubs. Rare version sold in 2009......................................£950
908	1962	**Mighty Antar & Transformer,** yellow cab/grey low loader/red ramps with transformer load. Yellow picture lift-off lid box, 2 inner packing pieces, transformer accessories sealed in polybag & separate assembly instructions...£1,000

943 Foden Octopus ESSO Tanker, dk red, mint in excellent blue/white stripe box. Sold for £440 DJ Auctions

944 Foden Octopus SHELL BP Tanker, yellow/white, mint in pictorial end flap box. Sold for £300 DJ Auctions

900 SERIES GUYS

Introduced in 1954 these 900 series Guys all had 2nd type cabs with the bracket to either side of the number plate and all came in blue/white stripe lift-off lid boxes.

Prices below are for mint boxed models.

911	1954	**Guy 4 Ton Lorry** (formerly 431 & 511)	
		Mid blue cab, chassis, back & hubs	£1,400
		Violet blue cab & chassis. Mid blue back & hubs	£190
912	1954	**Guy Flat Truck** (formerly 432 & 512)	
		Mid blue cab, chassis & hubs. Red back	£240
913	1954	**Guy Flat Truck with Tailboard** (formerly 433 & 513).	
		Violet cab & chassis. Orange back. Mid blue hubs.	£160
		Orange cab & chassis. Green back & hubs. Model numbered 513 but packed in blue/white stripe box numbered 913 picturing all green model	£1,200
914	1965	**AEC Articulated Lorry**, red cab with BRS decal. Colour picture box	£110
915	1973	**AEC with Flat Trailer**. Bubble pack.	
		Orange cab	£50
		Blue cab	£90
		White cab THAMES BOARD PAPER MILLS promotional, each stamped UNILINER	£3,600
917	1954	**SPRATTS Guy Van** (formerly 514) cream/red. Blue/white stripe box	£400
917	1968	**Mercedes Truck & Trailer,** blue cab version (non advertising). Colour picture box with inner diarama tray.	
		Blue cab, yellow trailers, white covers	£70
		Blue cab, yellow trailers, blue covers	£190
		Green cab HENRY JOHNSON promotional in plain white card box	£380
918	1955	**EVER READY Guy Truck** (1st & 2nd type cab versions), blue. Blue/white stripe box	£640
919	1957	**GOLDEN SHRED Guy Van** (2nd type cab), red. Blue/white stripe box	£520
920	1960	**HEINZ Guy Warrior Van,** red with ketchup bottle design. Unillustrated blue/white striped box.	£2,700
921	1954	**Bedford Articulated Truck,** yellow cab. Blue/white stripe box	£90
922	1954	**Big Bedford Lorry** (formerly 408 & 521), maroon cab version	£80
		* Add £50 to price guide for blue cab version	
923	1955	**HEINZ Guy Warrior Van,** red with Baked Beans can design. Illustrated blue/white striped box.	£240

Rare 934 Leyland Octopus Wagon, Dk blue/yellow, red hubs, mint in excellent blue/white stripe box. Sold for £3000 DJ Auctions

934 Leyland Octopus Wagon, yellow/mid green, red hubs, mint in excellent blue/white stripe box. Sold for £190 DJ Auctions

Ref.	First Issued	Model	TPG
930	1960	**Bedford Pallet Jekta Van** with 3 pallets, orange/yellow with Dinky & Meccano livery. Blue/white striped box with internal card packaging...£340	
931	1954	**Leyland Comet Lorry with Stake Body** (formerly 417 & 531), violet cab. Blue/white stripe box..£160	
932	1954	**Leyland Comet Lorry with Hinged Tailboard** (formerly 418 & 532), blue & green cab versions. Blue/white stripe box ....£110-140 * Add £200 to price guide for red cab version	
933	1954	**Leyland Comet Cement Wagon** (formerly 419 & 533), yellow with PORTLAND BLUE CIRCLE CEMENT decal. Blue/white stripe box £160	
934	1956	**Leyland Octopus Wagon,** yellow cab version. Blue/white striped box. Blue cab, yellow rear, red hubs, blue/white stripe box ....£2,800 Yellow cab, green rear, red hubs, blue/white stripe box £360	
935	1964	**Leyland Octopus Flat Truck with Chains,** 8 posts. Dk blue cab, grey rear, grey hubs, colour lift off lid picture box ....£3,200 Mid green cab, grey rear, red hubs, colour lift off lid picture box £1,500	
936	1964	**Leyland 8 Wheel Chassis with 5 ton weights,** red/silver with 'Another Leyland on Test' decal. Colour lift off lid picture box £90	
940	1977	**Mercedes Benz LP1920 Truck,** white cab version. Window box ....£25 Orange cab Pre production LAND LINK EUROPA...£580 White FISONS promotional, window box ....£500 Military green promotional model..£320	
941	1956	**MOBILGAS Foden 14 Ton Tanker** (2nd type), red. Blue/white stripe lift off lid box.............£190	
942	1955	**REGENT Foden 14 Ton Tanker** (2nd type), red/white/blue. Blue/white stripe lift off lid box.....£750	
943	1958	**ESSO Foden 14 Ton Tanker** (2nd type), red. Blue/white stripe lift off lid box.........................£380	
944	1963	**Leyland Octopus SHELL-BP Tanker,** white/yellow cab versions. Colour lift off lid picture box. ..£170 White CORN PRODUCTS promotional model in plain white lift-off lid box £6,800	
945	1966	**AEC ESSO Fuel Tanker,** white cab. Bubble packed or colour picture box. ....£40 LUCAS OIL promotional...£120	
948	1961	**Tractor Trailer** in either McLEAN or ROADWAY DOVER EXPRESS livery, red cab. Blue/white stripe box...£140	
950	1978	**Foden Fuel Tanker red cab,** white tank. Red/blue window box, polystyrene inner tray & block between cab & tank Burmah decals...£40 Shell decals £50	

935 Leyland Octopus Flat Truck with Chains, mid green/grey, red hubs, mint in scuffed yellow pictorial box. Sold for £1600 DJ Auctions

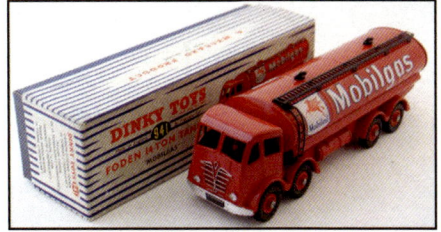

941 Foden Type 2 14 Ton MOBILGAS Tanker, red, mint in excellent blue/white stripe box. Sold for £800 DJ Auctions

951	1954	**Trailer** (formerly 428 & 551), grey. £10-15	
		Supplied to retailers in blue, orange/white label trade boxes of 3. Price for complete box £45	
958	1961	**Guy Warrior Snow Plough,** yellow/black body version. Blue/white striped box	
		Blue/white striped lift-off lid box..£130	
		Illustrated yellow lift-off lid box £170	
967	1959	**BBC TV Control Room,** green. Blue/white stripe lift-off lid box £140	
968	1959	**BBC TV Roving Eye Vehicle with cameraman,** camera & detachable aerial, green.	
		Blue/white stripe lift-off lid box..£140	
969	1959	**BBC TV Extending Mast Vehicle,** green, silver mast & plastic antenna. Blue/white stripe	
		lift-off lid box...£200	
970	1967	**Jones Bedford TK Fleetmaster Crane,** red & yellow cab versions. Colour picture box with	
		internal packing card & ring	
		Chrome button hubs with chrome hook £110	
		Red plastic hubs with black hook £110	
971	1954	**Coles Mobile Crane** (formerly 571) with driver, yellow/black. Blue/white stripe lift off lid box....£40	
972	1955	**Coles 20 Ton Mounted Crane,** yellow/orange & yellow/black versions. Colour picture &	
		Blue/whited striped lift off lid box versions. £120	
		Orange/yellow version in promotional 16th INTERNATIONAL COMMERCIAL MOTOR	
		SHOW labelled box..£320	
973	1954	**Goods Yard Crane** (formerly 752), yellow on blue base. Blue/white stripe box.......................£35	
974	1968	**AEC Hoynor Car Transporter,** blue cab versions. Colour picture box £80	
977	1960	**Servicing Platform Vehicle,** red/cream body. Blue/white stripe box...........................£120	
978	1964	**Bedford TK Refuse Wagon,** green cab versions. Colour picture lift-off lid box. £50	
		* Expect to pay £20 for later window box version	
979	1961	**NEWMARKET Racehorse Transport,** 2-tone grey/yellow with decal. Blue/white stripe box.£540	
981	1954	**BRITISH RAILWAYS horsebox** (formerly 581), maroon with decal. Blue/white stripe box...£160	
982	1955	**Pullmore Car Transporter** (formerly 582), glazed & unglazed, dk blue cab, lt blue transporter.	
		Blue/white stripe box showing loading ramp. £120	
		Later mid blue cab version £500	
983	1958	**DINKY AUTO SERVICE Car Carrier & Trailer,** red with grey ramps. Blue/white stripe box ..£260	
985	1958	**DINKY AUTO SERVICE Car Carrier Trailer,** red with grey ramps. Blue/white stripe box	
		with 2 inner packing pieces...£120	

968 BBC TV Roving Eye Vehicle complete with cameraman & roof aerial, excellent boxed condition. Sold for £90 Wallis & Wallis

982 Pullmore Car Transporter, mid blue cab VG in good blue/white stripe box with 984 loading ramp. Sold for £60 Aston's

Ref.	First Issued	Model	TPG
986	1959	**Mighty Antar with Propeller,** red cab, grey trailer with bronze propellor load. Blue/white stripe box with internal packing pieces	£240
987	1962	**ABC TELEVISION Control Room,** camera & operator figure, blue/grey. Yellow picture lift-off lid box	£170
988	1962	**ABC TV Transmitter Van,** roof mounted dish, blue/grey. Yellow picture lift-off lid box with inner card protective ring	£150
989	1963	**AUTO TRANSPORTERS Car Transporter,** yellow cab. Yellow picture lift-off lid box	£2,900
991	1948	**Trailer** (formerly 551), grey version. Unboxed	£15
991	1954	**SHELL CHEMICALS AEC Tanker,** red/yellow. Blue/white stripe box	£120

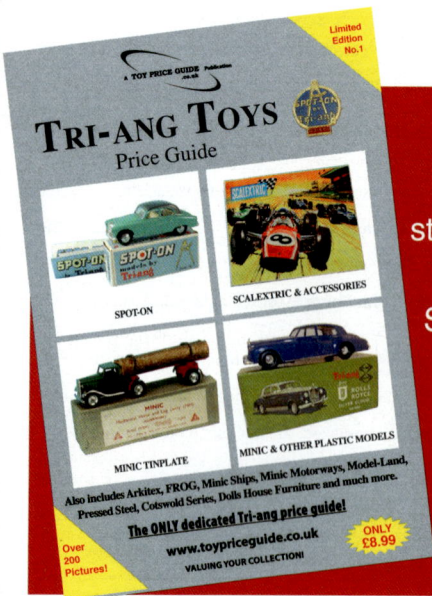

942 Foden Type 2 14 Ton REGENT Tanker, dk blue/ red, mint in excellent blue/white stripe box. Sold for £500 DJ Auctions

986 Mighty Antar Low Loader with Propeller Load, VG, tear to box lid. Sold for £100 Wallis & Wallis

GIFT SETS

1	1946	**Commercial Vehicles Set;** 29c Bus, 25b Wagon, 25d Tanker, 25e Tipper & 25f Market Gardeners Truck. Blue grained lid with picture label or green marble effect box with blue/white label £2,300
2	1952	**Commercial Vehicles Set;** 25m Bedford Tipper, 27d Land Rover, 30n Farm Produce Wagon, 30p Tanker, 30s Austin Wagon. Blue/white stripe box £1,200
6	1946	**Commercial Vehicles Set;** 29b Streamlined Bus, 29c Double Decker, 25h Fire Engine, 30e Breakdown Truck, 30f Ambulance. Blue box with yellow/blue label. US issue £1,600
12	1937	**Postal Set 6pce set including 34b Royal Mail Van.** Grey/blue box with yellow insert............£560
25	1934	**Commercial Motor Vehicle Set;** 25a Wagon, 25b Covered Wagon, 25c Flat Truck, 25d ESSO Tanker, 25e Tipper & 25f Market Gardener Truck. Blue grained effect lid with colour picture label...£2,100
25	1934	**Commercial Motor Vehicle Set;** 25b Covered Wagon, 25d POOL Tanker, 25e Tipper & 25f Market Gardener Truck; 25g Trailer, 25h Fire Engine. Blue grained effect lid with colour picture label £2,700
28	1934	**Delivery Vans Set (1st type)** including 6 vehicles produced 1934-1935; HORNBY, PICKFORDS, MANCHESTER GUARDIAN, OXO, ENSIGN CAMERAS, PALETHORPES. Yellow printed box £30,000
28	1936	**Delivery Vans Set (2nd type)** including 6 vehicles produced 1936-40; SWAN, EXIDE, FRY'S, OSRAM, HOVIS, OVALTINE. Yellow printed box £2,700
33	1935	**Mechanical Horse & 5 Trailer Set;** 33a mechanical Horse, 33b Flat Truck, 33c Open Wagon, 33d Box Van, 33e Dust Wagon & 33f Petrol Tank. Blue grain box with colour label £1,100
33	1935	**Mechanical Horse & 4 Trailer Set;** 33a mechanical Horse, 33b Flat Truck, 33c Open Wagon, 33d Box Van & 33e Dust Wagon. Green grain box with colour label...£800
299	1957	**Post Office Services set;** 260 Morris Van, 261 GPO Van, 750 Telephone box plus 2 figures. Blue/white stripe box with diorama insert...£400
990	1956	**Car Transporter Set;** 982 Pullmore, 154 Hillman, 156 Rover, 161 Austin, 162 Zephyr & boxed ramp. Blue/white striped box with inner card packing piece...£500

960 Albion Concrete Mixer, grey wheels, black
plastic hubs in VG condition within fair picture
lift-off lid box. Sold for £80 Special Auction Services

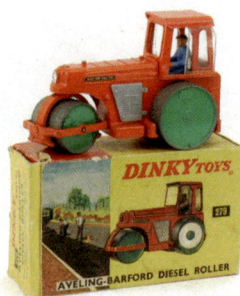

979 Aveling Barford Road Roller, excellent in
a fair box missing an end flap.
Sold for £45 Special Auction Services

Ref.	First Issued	Model		TPG

CONSTRUCTION

25p	1948	**Aveling Barford Road Roller** (later renumbered 251), green. Unboxed	£25
		Supplied in trade box of 4. Price for 1 model in trade box sold in 2009	£70
		Orange version sold in 2000	£180
251	1954	**Aveling Barford Road Roller,** green (2 shades). Yellow illustrated box	£40
279	1965	**Aveling Barford Diesel Roller,** driver, orange, blue or green rollers. Yellow picture box.	£50
380	1977	**Skip Truck**, yellow/orange. Window box	£20
382	1978	**Dumper Truck.** Window box	£20
419	1956	**Leyland Comet Cement Lorry** (later renumbered 933), PORTLAND BLUE CIRCLE CEMENT, yellow body. Yellow lift-off lid box	£200
437	1962	**Muir Hill 2WL Loader,** red, yellow & orange versions. Lift-off lid, bubble pack & window box versions.	£30
561	1949	**Blaw Know Bulldozer** (later renumbered 961), red, black or green rubber tracks. Blue, orange/white label box	£45
562	1948	**Muir Hill Dump Truck** (later renumbered 962), yellow. Blue label box	£25
924	1972	**Aveling Barford Centaur Dump Truck,** red/yellow. Colour picture box	£40
925	1965	**Leyland Dump Truck,** white cab with SAND BALLAST GRAVEL decal on tailgate. Colour picture box	£140
961	1953	**Blaw Know Bulldozer (**formerly 561). Blue/white stripe box	
	1954	Red, black tracks	£45
	1953	Yellow, green tracks	£60
	1961	Orange plastic body	£180
959	1961	**Foden Dump Truck & Bulldozer,** red cab	
		Red cab, red back. Colour picture box.	£150
		Red cab, red back. Yellow picture lift off lid box.	£340
		Red cab, silver back. Yellow picture lift off lid box.	£260
960	1960	**Albion Concrete Mixer Lorry,** orange. Blue/white striped box	£120
961	1954	**Blaw Know Bulldozer,** driver, rubber tracks, red & yellow version. Blue/white stripe lift off lid box.	£45
		* Orange plastic body version sold for £180	

970 Jones Fleetmaster Cantilever Crane, red with chrome button hubs, excellent in a good pictorial box. Sold for £65 Aston's

752 Goods Yard Crane, VG boxed condition. Sold for £35 Toy Price Guide archive

962	1954	**Muir Hill Dumper** (formerly 563), yellow. Yellow picture lift off lid box.	£35
963	1973	**Road Grader,** yellow/red & white/yellow versions. Bubble pack	£30
965	1955	**EUCLID Dump Truck,** yellow body. Blue/white striped box	£70
965	1969	**TEREX Rear Dump Truck,** yellow. Colour picture & yellow picture box versions	£540
966	1960	**Marrel Multi Bucket Unit,** yellow with grey skip. Blue/white stripe box	£100
967	1973	**Muir Hill Loader with driver,** yellow/red & orange/black versions. Bubble pack	£25
973	1971	**Eaton YALE Tractor Shovel,** yellow, red/yellow & yellow red body versions. Colour picture box	£30
975	1963	**RUSTON BUCYRUS Excavator,** yellow with red jib/bucket. Yellow white display box	£180
976	1968	**MICHIGAN Tractor Dozer,** driver, yellow/red body. Colour picture box	£35
977	1973	**Shovel Dozer,** yellow/red with either silver or black tracks. Bubble packed	£30
980	1972	**Coles 150T Hydra Truck,** yellow & orange versions. Colour picture box with inner packaging.	£50
		200mm x 135mm window poster for above model. Sold in 2006	£30
	1976	SPARROWS CRANE HIRE promotional issue	£220
984	1974	**Atlas Digger,** red/yellow with black or yellow arm. Colour picture box	£35

GIFT SETS

010	1962	**Road Maintenance Staff** (35mm) plastic figure set containing 6 workmen, hut, wheelbarrow, brazier & 3 lamps, plastic transfer sheet. Yellow window box including plastic transfer sheet	£60
399	1977	**Convoy Set;** 380 Skip Truck, 381 Truck & 382 Dumper. Window box	£30
778	-	**Road Repair Warning Boards,** 6pce set blister packed on yellow card	£30
900	1964	**Site Building Set;** 437 Loader, 960 Albion Mixer, 961 Bulldozer (plastic issue), 962 Dumper, 965 Euclid Dump Truck. Grey/red/yellow hinged lid box with inner tray	£1,400

Gift Set 695 7.2 Howitzer & Tractor, missing driver otehwise VG in a good box. Sold for £165 Special Auction Services

642 Pressure Refueller in RAF blue, excellent, good in good blue/white stripe box. Sold for £45 Aston's

MILITARY

22f	1933	**Army Tank,** MECCANO, HORNBY SERIES or DINKY TOYS cast inside pre war issues. Unboxed	
	pre war	Lead body, red or white tracks, grey or green with orange turret versions..................................£170	
	post war	Diecast body, black rubber tracks, brown or green versions..£60	
22s	1939	**Searchlight Lorry,** gloss & matt green versions. Unboxed £480	
		Trade box for 6 models containing 2 models. Sold in 2009 ....£1,200	
37c	1937	**Royal Signal Despatch Rider,** khaki rider on green motorbike, white or black tyres. Unboxed£40	
		Rare military green version painted all over except face. Sold in 2008 ....£260	
		Complete Trade Box (yellow) containing 6 models. Sold in 2009 ....£320	
		Blue Presentation box containing 6 models. Sold in 2009 ....£400	
109	1976	**Pre-production Land Rover in military green,** black plastic wheels & plastic baseplate. Sold in 2008..£160	
139a	1952	**U.S. Army Ford Fordor Staff Car,** green, white roof star roof decal. Unboxed..........................£100	
		Supplied to retailers in trade boxes of 6. Sold in 2006 ....£380	
151a	1937	**Medium Tank,** chain track & rubber wheel versions. Unboxed £50-70	
151b	1937	**6 Wheel Covered Wagon** Unboxed. £160	
151c	1937	**Cooker Trailer.** Unboxed...£30-40	
151d	1937	**Water Tank Trailer.** Unboxed £30-40	
152a	1937	**Light Tank,** chain tracks & rubber wheel versions. Unboxed £50	
		Supplied to retailers in trade boxes of 6. Price for a single model in a trade box £340	
152b	1937	**Reconnaissance Car,** 6 wheels, miliray green. Unboxed...£45	
		Olive drab US export issue..£110	
152c	1937	**Austin Seven.** Unboxed £40	
153a	1946	**Jeep,** green & brown versions, white star on bonnet. Unboxed £50-60	
161a	1939	**6 Wheel Covered Wagon with mounted Searchlight** (151b casting). Unboxed	
		Matt green version...£100	
		Gloss green version £480	
161b	1939	**Anti-Aircraft Gun & Trailer,** green & brown versions. Unboxed.	
		Matt green version...£80	
		Gloss green version £180	

642 RAF Pressure Refueller, grey blue, mint in mint blue/white stripe box. Sold for £130 DJ Auctions

616 AEC Artic Transporter with Chieftain Tank, excellent, complete with netting in a good box. Sold for £85 Aston's

162a	1939	**Light Dragon Tractor with chain tracks,** green. Unboxed	£100
162b	1939	**Ammunition Trailer.** Unboxed	£20-30
162c	1939	**18 Pounder gun.** Unboxed	£20-30
170m	1954	**Ford Fordor Sedan U.S. Army Staff Car,** without star. Unboxed	£120
281	1973	**ARMY Hovercraft with gunner figure.** Window box	£30-40
601	1966	**Austin Paramoke,** brown & grey versions. Picture box or bubble packaging versions	£50-60
604	1976	**Bomb Disposal Land Rover,** 'Explosive Disposal' decal, robot kit on sprue. Window box with header card	£50-60
609	1974	**105mm Howitzer & Crew.** Bubble packed	£25-35
612	1973	**Commando Jeep.** Window box & bubble packaging versions	£30-40
620	1971	**Berliet Missile Launcher.** Picture box & bubble pack versions	£125-150
621	1954	**3 Ton Army Wagon.** Yellow picture box	£50-60
622	1954	**10 Ton Army Truck.** Blue/white stripe Supertoys box	£50
622	1975	**Bren Gun Carrier.** Window box & bubble pack versions	£20-30
623	1954	**Army Covered Wagon.** Yellow picture box	£40-50
624	1955	**Daimler Military Ambulance** (formerly 30h), green with red cross on sides. Unboxed	£80-100
625	1975	**Six Pounder Gun with shells on 2 plastic sprues.** Bubble pack	£15-20
626	1956	**Military Ambulance,** cream with red crosses. Yellow picture box	£45-55
		* Increase price guide by £20 for glazed window version	
630	1973	**Ferret Armoured Car,** green. Bubble pack	£20-25
641	1954	**1 Ton Army Cargo Truck,** glazed and unglazed window versions. Yellow picture box & yellow/red box versions	£40-50
642	1957	**RAF Pressure Refueller.** Plain card with blue label & blue/white stripe box versions	£100-130
643	1958	**Army Water Tanker,** glazed and unglazed window versions. Yellow picture box	£40-50
651	1954	**Centurion Tank,** olive green. Dinky & Supertoys picture box versions.	£65-80
		* For later issues with plastic rollers add £50 to price guide	
654	1973	**155mm Mobile Gun with 4 plastic shells.** Bubble pack	£20-25
		20x15cm window poster for above model. Sold in 2006	£30

661 Recovery Tractor, khaki green, driver, mint in mint blue/white stripe box complete with inner packaging. Sold for £110 DJ Auctions

U.S. issue 674 Austin Champ, white, olive green mudguards, late style plastic hubs, correct seats with no holes for personnel to be fitted, mint unboxed. Sold for £180 Wallis & Wallis

Ref.	First Issued	Model	TPG
656	1975	**88mm Gun with 6 plastic shells.** Bubble pack	£20-25
660	1956	**Mighty Antar Tank Transporter**, green. Dinky & Supertoys picture lift-off lid box versions	£90-120
660a	1978	**Anti Aircraft Gun & Crew.** Bubble pack	£20-25
661	1957	**Recovery Tractor with mounted crane.** Supertoys picture box.	£90-110
		* Add £50 to price guide for plastic wheel version	
662	1975	**88mm Gun & Crew.** Bubble pack	£20-25
665	1964	**Honest John Missile Launcher with grey or white missile.** Dinky & Supertoys picture box versions.	£140
		* Reduce price guide by £40 for bubble pack version	
		200mm x 135mm window poster for above model. Sold in 2007	£35
666	1959	**Missile Erector Vehicle & Corporal Missile Launcher with white/black missile.** Blue/white stripe Supertoys box	£190
667	1960	**Missile Servicing Platform.** Blue/white stripe Supertoys box	£170
667	1976	**Armoured Patrol Car.** Window box with header card	£25-30
668	1976	**Foden Army Truck.** Window box with header card	£40-50
670	1954	**Armoured Car.** Yellow picture box	£30-40
673	1953	**Scout Car.** Yellow picture box	£30-40
674	1954	**Austin Champ, green.** Yellow picture box.	£45-55
		* Add £200 to price guide for white U.N. issue	
675	1955	**Ford Sedan Army Staff Car,** green with miliary star decal. Yellow picture box	£160
676	1955	**Armoured Personnel Carrier.** Yellow picture box	£30-40
676a	1973	**Daimler Armoured Car**, later Speedwheels version. Bubble pack	£25-30
677	1957	**Armoured Command Vehicle.** Yellow picture box	£50-60
680	1972	**Ferret Armoured Car,** brown. Bubble packed	£20-30
		Plastic pre-production model, finished in green with black Speedwheels in standard issue bubble pack	£50
681	1972	**DUKW Armoured Vehicle,** blue or green versions. Bubble pack	£20-25
		Plastic pre-production model, green, F17 decal, black Speedwheels. Bubble pack	£50

651 Centurian Tank, mint in excellent blue/white stripe box. Sold for £55 Aston's

661 Recovery Tractor, khaki green, driver, mint in mint blue/white stripe box complete with inner packaging. Sold for £110 DJ Auctions

682	1972	**Stalwart Load Carrier,** Speedwheels. Bubble pack £20-25
		20cm x 15cm window poster for above model. Sold in 2006 ....£35
		Plastic pre-production model, finished in green with black Speedwheels no packaging £50
683	1972	**Chieftain Tank,** green with plastic shells. Window box & bubble packaging versions £30-40
		20x15cm window poster for above model. Sold in 2006 ....£40
686	1957	**25 Pounder Field Gun.** Yellow picture box £10-20
687	1957	**25 Pounder Trailer.** Unboxed £5-10
		Supplied to retailers in trade boxes of 6. Price for a complete trade box £70
687	1978	**Convoy Army Truck.** Window box with header card £20-30
688	1957	**Field Artillery Tractor.** Yellow picture box £30-40
689	1957	**Medium Artillery Tractor.** Blue/white stripe lift-off lid box. £90
		* Add £30 to price guide for scarcer colour picture lift-off lid box
690	1974	**Scorpion Tank,** camoflauge netting, plastic shells & decal sheet. Window box & bubble
		pack box versions £30-40
691	1974	**Striker Anti Tank with plastic tracks & missiles.** Window box & bubble pack box versions £25-35
692	1955	**5.5 Medium Gun.** Yellow picture box £20-30
692	1974	**Leopard Tank,** grey with German decals & 6 shells on sprue. Bubble packed £60-70
693	1958	**7.2 Howitzer Gun.** Yellow picture box..£25-35
694	1975	**Hanomog Tank Destroyer,** grey with German decals. Bubble packed......................................£50-60
696	1975	**Leopard Anti Tank Aircraft,** grey with German decals & 12 shells on sprues. Bubble packed....£50-60
699	1975	**Leopard Recovery Tank,** grey with German decals. Bubble packed £50-60

GIFT SETS

1	1954	**Military Vehicles Set** (later renumbered 699); 621 3 Ton Wagon, 641 1 Ton Truck, 674 Austin
		Champ & 676 Armoured Car. Blue/white stripe box £500-600
5	1953	**Military Vehicles Set**; 151a Tank, 151b Transport Wagon, 152b Reconnaisance Car, 53a Jeep,
		161b & Gun. Blue/white stripe box £2250-2500
150	1937	**Royal Tanks Corps Personnel 6pce set** comprising; officer, 2 x privates (seated), 2 x private
		(standing), driver & NCO. Yellow & blue lift-off lid box versions..£170
151	1937	**Medium Tank Set;** 150d Driver, 151a Tank, 151b Wagon, 151c Cooker Trailer & 151d Trailer. Blue
		box with diorama card insert £280

674 Austin Champ, khaki green, driver, mint in excellent red/yellow box. Sold for £70 DJ Auctions

Gift Set 697 25 Pounder Field Gun Set, mint in illustrated yellow lift-off lid box. S old for £155 DJ Auctions

Ref.	First Issued	Model	TPG
152	1937	**Light Tank Set;** 150d Driver, 152a Tank, 152 Reconnaissance Car & 152c Austin. Blue label box	..£220
156	1939	**Mechanised Army Set;** 151 Medium Tank, 151b 6 Wheeled Covered Wagon, 151c Cooker Trailer, 151d Searchlight Lorry, 161b Aircraft Gun with 2 figures, 152a Light Tank, 152c Austin Car, 152b Reconaissance Car, 162a Light Dragon Tractor, 162b trailer & 162c Quick Firing Gun in grey lift-off lid box with inner card stand	£1,000
161	1939	**Mobile Anti Aircraft Unit;** 161a Searchlight Lorry & 161b Trailer Gun. Green label box	..£400-500
162	1939	**Field Gun Set;** 162a Dragon Tractor, 162b Trailer & 162c Gun. Blue label box	£90
303	1978	**Commando Sqaud Set;** 687 Truck, 667 Car & 732 Helicopter. Window box	£60
603	1957	**Army Private,** box of 12 seated figures (diecast). Yellow lift-off lid box. * Reduce price guide by £40 for 1960s plastic version	£75
603a	1968	**Army Personnel Set,** box of 6 seated figures (diecast). * For later 1960s plastic version same price guide applies	£25
607	1957	**Field Gun Set;** 162a Dragon Tractor, 162b Trailer & 162c Gun. Blue/white stripe box label box	....£100
615	1968	**U.S. Jeep & 105mm Howitzer.** Picture box with diorama card tray & bubble pack versions	.....£75
616	1976	**AEC Transporter & Tank;** 974 Transporter, 683 Chieftain Tank & netting. Picture box	£60
617	1967	**VW KDF & 50mm gun.** Colour picture box & bubble pack versions	£70
618	1976	**AEC Transporter & Helicopter;** 974 Transporter, 724 Helicopter & netting. Window box	£65
619	1976	**Bren Gun Carrier Set;** 622 Carrier & 625 6pdr Gun. Bubble pack	£45
677	1972	**Task Force Set;** 680 Armoured Car, DUKW & 682 Stalwart Carrier. Bubble packed on card tray	.....£70
695	1962	**Howitzer & Tractor;** 689 Tractor & 693 Gun. Picture lift off lid box with inner card stand	£280
697	1957	**Field Gun Set;** 688 Tractor, 687 Trailer & 686 25pdr Gun. Yellow lift off lid box with plain inner card tray	£80
698	1957	**Tank Transporter Set;** 660 Mighty Antar & 651 Centurion Tank. Blue/white stripe box	£220
699	1955	**Military Vehicles Set;** 621 Wagon, 641 Truck, 674 Austin Champ & 676 Armoured Car. Blue/white striped box	£320

Rare export issues of 271 Motorcycle Patrol; TS livery for the Belgian market and ANWB version for the Dutch market, both in VG unboxed condition. Sold for £120 Wallis & Wallis

37c pre-war Royal Signals Dispatch Rider, fully restored, unboxed. Sold for £20 DJ Auctions

MOTOR CYCLES

Prices below are for unboxed models (originally in Trade Box containing 6 models)

37a	1937	**Civilian Motor Cycle** (later renumbered 41)	£30-40
		Complete Trade Box. Sold in 2010	£300
		White rider version	£70
37b	1937	**Police Motor Cycle** (later renumbered 42), black with dk blue rider	£30-40
37c	1937	**Royal Signals Despatch Rider,** green, khaki rider	£40-50
		Trade box containing 6 models. Sold in 2009	£320
42b	1935	**Police Motor Cycle Patrol & Sidecar** (later renumbered 43)	£40-50
43b	1935	**RAC Motor Cycle Patrol,** blue/black with blue/black rider, black or white tyres (see military section)	£30-40
44b	1935	**AA Motor Cycle Patrol** (later renumbered 270), black/yellow with brown rider	£40-50
		Trade box containing 6 models. Sold in 2006	£320

GIFT SETS

37	1937	**Motor Cycles Set** containing 37a Civilian, 37b Police & 37c Despatch Rider. Blue box	£380
37a	1937	**Motor Cycles Set** containing 6 civilian motor cycles each in a different colour all with solid white tyres. Blue box with inner card diorama. US issue	£1,200
43	1935	**4pce RAC Set** including; 43a tin plate RAC box, 43b Motor Cycle Patrol, 43c RAF Guide directing traffic & 43d RAC Guide saluting. Blue box with inner card diorama	£420
44	1937	**4pce AA Set** including; 44a tin plate AA box, 44b Motor Cycle Patrol, 44c AA Guide directing traffic & 44d AA Guide saluting. Blue box with inner card diorama	£260

103 Captain Scarlet Spectrum Patrol Car, mint in good pictorial box complete with scarce 1968 72569 folded leaflet. Sold for £150 Aston's

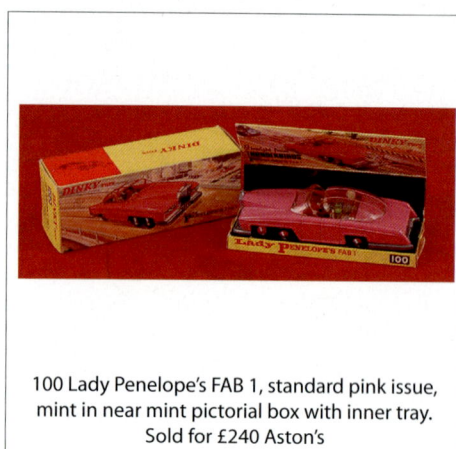

100 Lady Penelope's FAB 1, standard pink issue, mint in near mint pictorial box with inner tray. Sold for £240 Aston's

TV & FILM RELATED

Ref.	First Issued	Model	
100	1967	**Thunderbirds Lady Penelope's FAB1,** pink, with clear plastic sliding roof.	
		Pink version, clear canopy, picture card box, inner tray diorama	£180
		Rare fluorescent pink version, striped canopy, picture card box, inner tray diorama	£280
		Pink version, clear canopy, bubble pack, missiles & harpoons in factory sealed polybag	£260
101	1967	**Thunderbirds II & IV,** central pod containing plastic vehicle, spring loaded legs.	
		Green, picture card box, inner diorama card tray	£240
		Blue/green, picture card box, inner diorama card tray	£180
		Gloss green picture card box, inner diorama card tray	£390
		Green or blue green version, bubble pack	£110
102	1969	**Joe's Car,** green includes lapel badge & folded instruction leaflet.	
		Picture card box with diorama card tray including instruction leaflet.	£200
		Bubble pack version (battery operated issue)	£120
103	1968	**Captain Scarlet Spectrum Patrol Car**	
		Metallic red, coloure picture box, packing ring & instruction leaflet	£110
		Metallic gold, bubble pack	£280
		Metallic bronze, bubble pack	£90
		Metallic red, bubble pack	£75
		Resin pre-production model in yellow sold in 2000	£600
104	1968	**Captain Scarlet Spectrum Pursuit Vehicle,** 2 missiles, blue with folded instruction leaflet	
		Picture card box, card diorama inner tray with hanging side door Cpt Scarlet figure	£160
		Bubble pack with fixed side door Cpt Scarlet figure	£110
105	1968	**Maximum Security Vehicle with radioactive crate & decal sheet,** white with blue or red interior. Picture box	£140
106	1967	**Prisoner Mini Moke,** white with red/white striped canopy, bicycle decal . Picture box	£180
106	1977	**Thunderbirds II & IV,** central pod containing plastic vehicle, spring loaded legs, blue.	
		Bubble pack	£140
		Window box	£100
107	1967	**Stripey the Magic Mini,** 2 seated figures & 2 Bearanda's, red/white/blue/yellow striped car.	
		Picture box with inner diorama card tray	£240
108	1969	**Sam's Car,** WIN badge & instructions	£90-130
		Metallic red, yellow inner, picture box, inner diorama tray	£130
		Lt blue, yellow inner, picture box, inner diorama tray	£130
		Chrome, yellow inner, picture box, inner diorama tray	£120

106 The Prisoner Mini Moke, VG condition in a torn box. Sold for £130 Aston's

104 Captain Scarlet Spectrum Pursuit Vehicle, excellent in sellotape repaired blister. Sold for £85 Aston's

109	1969	**Gabriel's Model T Ford,** 2 seated figures, yellow/black. Picture box with diorama card tray .£70
111	1976	**Cinderella's Coach,** 8 horses & riders, Window box £25
		Pre-production model finished in gold with pink interior, 4 white horses £70
112	1978	**Purdey's TR7 with Speed Wheels,** bonnet decal, yellow. Window box. £30
113	1978	**Pre-production model of John Steed's Jaguar XJ5.3C,** blue with Steed figure. Only 36 of these models were made £1,200
350	1970	**Tiny's Mini Moke,** giraffe's head protruding through roof, red. Colour picture box with diorama inner tray & single inner packing piece £150
351	1971	**UFO Interceptor,** green with front missile & plastic ski's. Picture box with diorama card tray £140
		Window box with polystyrene inner tray........................£100
		Pre-production model in blue sold in 2007........................£320
352	1971	**Ed Straker's Car,** gold & yellow versions. Colour picture box & bubble pack version..............£70
353	1971	**SHADO 2 Mobile,** green with brown or silver tracks. Picture box or bubble pack versions.
		Green, grey track, picture box, inner card packaging £160
		Green, black tracks, bubble pack £220
		Metallic blue, black tracks, window box with polystyrene inner tray £180
354	1972	**Pink Panther car,** flywheel & non flywheel versions. Picture card box & blister pack versions £40
		225mm x 180mm window poster for above model. Sold in 2006..................£40
		Yellow pre-production sample with red giro, no figure, fitted with Speedwheels sold in 200 £240
355	1972	**Lunar Roving Vehicle,** metallic blue with 2 seated astronaut figures. Bubble packed..............£35
		TIOXIDE promotional model, white blue label box........................£280
357	1977	**Klingon Battle Cruiser,** blue with 6 torpedo disks. Window box £30
358	1976	**USS Enterprise,** white with 6 torpedo disks. Window box £70
359	1975	**Eagle Transporter,** white/green with decal sheet.
		Bubble pack version........................£90
		Window box version........................£110
360	1975	**Eagle Freighter,** 6 radioactive drums, white/red & white/blue versions with decal sheet.
		Bubble pack version........................£110
		Window box version........................£130
		23cm x 12cm window poster for above model. Sold in 2006 ....£40
361	1978	**Zygon War Chariot,** 2 seated figures & 2 missiles, green. Window box. £30
361	1978	**Galactic War Chariot,** 2 seated figures & 2 missiles, blue. Window box £30

353 Shado 2 Mobile, scarce metallic blue version, mint in mint illustrated window box. Sold for £340 Aston's

108 Sam's Car, chrome, yellow interior complete with instructions and WIN badge, excellent in VG pictorial box. Sold for £120 Special Auction Services

Ref.	First Issued	Model	TPG
362	1978	**Trident Star Fighter,** 2 rockets, black/orange. Window box	£30
363	1979	**Zygon Patroller,** silver/blue. Window box	£30
364	1979	**NASA Space Shuttle with satellite,** white. Window box	£40
367	1979	**Space Battle Cruiser,** pilot figure, red/white. Window box	£25
368	1979	**Zygon Marauder,** 4 spacement, red/white. Window box	£20
371	1980	**USS Enterprise** (small version), white. Window box with plain tray	£25
372	1980	**Klingon Battle Cruiser** (small version), blue. Window box with plain tray	£25
477	1970	**Parsley's Car,** plastic lion figure, green/black. Picture box with inner diorama tray	£90
486	1965	**Dinky Beats Morris Oxford,** 3 figures, pink/green car. Window box on diorama card tray	£80
602	1976	**Armoured Command Car,** roof scanner, green & blue/green versions. Colour picture box & window box versions. * From Gerry Anderson's THE INVESTIGATOR series	£45
802	1980	**Klingon Battle Cruiser** (small version), blue. Bubble packed version of 372	£20
803	1980	**USS Enterprise** (small version), white. Bubble packed version of 371	£20

GIFT SET

Ref.	First Issued	Model	TPG
309	1978	**Star Trek Gift Set,** 357 Klingon Cruiser & 358 Enterprise. Window box	£90

051 Station Staff & 053 Passengers in plain green and maroon boxes. Sold for £55 Special Auction Services

RAILWAY

16z	1935	**Articulated Train,** 2-tone blue, gold & cream versions (made in France). Unboxed £150-200
17a	1934	**Locomotive,** black/maroon & black/green versions. Unboxed £100-125
17b	1934	**Tender,** green & maroon versions. Unboxed..£30-40
20a	1935	**Coach,** brown/cream & green/white versions. Unboxed £50-60
20b	1935	**Guards Van,** brown/cream or green/white versions. Unboxed £50-60
21a	1932	**Tank Locomotive,** HORNBY SERIES cast inside, red/blue. Unboxed £80-100
21b	1932	**Open Wagon,** HORNBY SERIES or DINKY TOYS cast inside, green & maroon versions. Unboxed..£50-60
21c	1932	**Crane Wagon,** HORNBY SERIES cast inside, green. Unboxed £50-60
21d	1932	**Tanker Wagon,** DINKY TOYS cast inside, red. Unboxed......................................£50-60
21e	1932	**Lumber Wagon,** HORNBY SERIES or DINKY TOYS cast inside, brown & yellow versions. Unboxed..£50-60
26	1934	**GWR Rail Car,** brown, red, green & yellow versions with cream roof. Unboxed £100-125
26z	1937	**Diesel Road Car,** yellow, blue, green, orange & red versions with cream roof (made in France). Unboxed..£90-110
27	1934	**Tram Car,** OVALTINE & LIPTONS versions, various colours. Unboxed £200-250
784	1972	**Yellow 0-4-0 pre-production model with red wagon** sold in 2009...................................£45

GIFT SETS

001	1954	**Station Staff** (35mm) 5pce figure set (formerly No.1). Green lift off lid box £90
003	1954	**Passengers** (35mm) 6pce figure set (formerly No.3). Green lift off lid box £90
004	1954	**Engineering Staff** (35mm) 5pce figure set (formerly No.4). Green lift off lid box.......£80
005	1954	**Train & Hotel Staff** (35mm) 5pce figure set (formerly No.5). Green lift off lid box £90
050	1961	**Railway Staff** (35mm) 12pce plastic figure set. Clear plastic box....................................£35
051	1954	**Station Staff** (35mm) 6pce plastic figure set (also 1001). Green box £30
052	1961	**Railway Passengers** (35mm) 12pce plastic figure set. Clear plastic box........................£30
053	1954	**Passengers** (35mm) 6pce figure set. Green box...£30

No.5 Train & Hotel Staff 5pce set, mint in
a VG green labelled box.
Sold for £90 Toy Price Guide Archive

No.18 Goods Train with maroon /black Loco and 3
green/red Wagons, VG in a fair gold marbled box.
Sold for £350 Special Auction Services

Ref.	First Issued	Model	TPG
054	1962	**Railway Station Personnel 12pce plastic figure set.** Clear plastic box	£30
1	1931	**Station Staff** (40mm) 6pce set, HORNBY SERIES or DINKY TOYS on base. Lift off picture lid box with yellow insert	£130
1	1939	**Station Staff** (35mm) 6pce set. Green 'Modelled Miniatures' lift off lid box	£130
1	1946	**Station Staff** (35mm) 5pce set (later renumbered 001). Green 'Modelled Miniatures' lift off lid box	£90
1	1934	**Railway Accessories Set,** tinplate luggage truck & 4 luggage items	£80
3	1932	**Railway Passengers** (40mm) 6pce figure set HORNBY SERIES or DINKY TOYS on base. Lift-off picture lid box with yellow insert	£190
3	1932	**Railway Passengers** (35mm) 6pce figure set HORNBY SERIES or DINKY TOYS on base. Green lift-off picture lid box	£140
3	1939	**Railway Passengers** (35mm) 6pce set. Green 'Modelled Miniatures' lift-off lid box	£90
3	1946	**Railway Passengers** (35mm) 6pce set (later renumbered 003). Green 'Modelled Miniatures' lift-off lid box	£90
4	1932	**Engineering Staff** (40mm) 6pce figure set, HORNBY SERIES or DINKY TOYS on base. Lift-off picture lid box with yellow insert	£130
4	1932	**Engineering Staff** (35mm) 6pce figure set, HORNBY SERIES or DINKY TOYS on base. Lift-off picture lid box with yellow insert	£130
4	1946	**Enginnering Staff** (35mm) 5pce figure set. Green 'Modelled Miniatures' lift-off lid box	£140
5	1932	**Train & Hotel Staff** (40mm) 5pce figure set. HORNBY SERIES or DINKY TOYS on base. Lift-off picture lid box with yellow insert	£260
5	1932	**Train & Hotel Staff** (35mm) 5pce figure set. HORNBY SERIES or DINKY TOYS on base. Lift-off picture lid box with yellow insert	£130
5	1939	**Train & Hotel Staff** (35mm) 5pce figure set. Green 'Modelled Miniatures' lift-off lid box	£140
5	1946	**Train & Hotel Staff** (35mm) 5pce figure set (later renumbered 005). Green 'Modelled Miniatures' lift-off lid box	£75
16	1936	**Silver Jubilee Set,** loco, 2 coaches, LNER cast inside, blue, green red & silver versions with white tyres. Lift-off lid box	£220
16	1937	**Streamlined Train Set** (re-issue of above but in a different box)	£180

Pre-war 16 Silver Jubilee Train Set, VG in a fair blue landscape inner box.
Sold for £200 Special Auction Services

16	-	**Streamlined Train Set** (later re-issues), LNER & BR issues. Brown box	£110
17	1934	**Passenger Train 4pce set** including; locomotive, tender & 2 carriages, white tyres. Lift off-lid box	£420
18	1934	**Tank Goods Train 4pce set** including; locomotive & 3 carriages, white tyres. Lift-off lid box	£270
19	1935	**Mixed Goods Train 4pce set** including; locomotive & 3 wagons, white tyres. Lift-off lid box	£320
20	1934	**Tank Passenger 4pce set** including; green/black locomotive, 2 carriages & guards van, white tyres. Lift-off lid box	£270
21	1932	**Hornby Train 5pce set** including; locomotive, crane wagon & 3 other wagons, white tyres. Red 'Hornby Series' box	£450-550
21	1934	**Modelled Miniatures 5pce set** including; locomotive, crane wagon & 3 other wagons, white tyres. Red 'Modelled Miniatures' box	£450-550
784	1972	**3pce Dinky Goods Train Set GER livery,** including locomotive & 2 wagons. Bubble pack	£15
798	1954	**3pce Express Passenger Train Set,** BR livery, including locomotive & 2 carriages, white tyres. Yellow lift-off lid picture box with yellow insert card	£90
1001	1952	**Station Staff** (35mm) 6pce figure set (also set No.51) Green box	£45
1003	1952	**Passengers** (35mm) 6pce figure set (also set No.53). Red or green box	£45

Dinky Toys Shop Display Sign (45cm x 19cm), VG condition. Sold for £200 Wallis & Wallis

Pre-war Dinky Dolly Varden Dolls House, 1937, timber and printed leather board. An extremely rare item sold for £550 Special Auction Services

French Citroen 2CV Fourgonnette van in yellow ANWB (Belgian AA) livery, excellent unboxed. Sold for £180 Wallis & Wallis

258 Ford Fairlane USA Police Car, good in a poor box. Sold for £65 Special Auction Services

273 RAC Mini Van, red interior, excellent in a good box. Sold for £110 Special Auction Services

Pre war no.48 Petrol Station, mint in an excellent box. Sold for £540 DJ Auctions

Halls Distemper Advertisment, replacement board otherwise VG unboxed.
Sold for £100 Special Auction Services

4 Action Kits; 2 x 1014 Hawker Hurricanes & 1042 Spitfire & 1043 SEPECAT Jaguar, mint unopened boxes. Sold for £120 Special Auction Services

ACTION KITS

Issued between 1971-77 these bare model castings (without numbered bases) came with screws, paint bottle and in some instances transfer sheet, blister packed in 'folder' type card pack with instructions printed on the inside. In many cases different colour paint bottles were issued with the same model as described below:

1001	1971	**Rolls Royce Pantom V,** blue, red & white paint	£20-25
1002	1971	**Volvo 1800s Coupe,** yellow	£20-25
1003	1971	**Volkswagen 1300,** white & red	£20-25
1004	1971	**Ford Escort Police Car,** blue & white paint, transfer sheet	£20-25
1006	1973	**Ford Escort Mexico,** red, transfer sheet	£30-35
1007	1971	**Jensen FF,** blue & red	£20-25
1008	1973	**Mercedes Benz 600,** green, red or yellow	£20-25
1009	1971	**Lotus F1 Racing Car,** green, transfers	£20-25
1012	1973	**Ferrari 312B2 Racing Car,** red, transfers	£30-35
1014	1975	**Beach Buggy,** blue	£10-15
1017	1971	**Routemaster Bus,** red, transfers	£20-25
1018	1974	**Leyland Atlantean Bus,** white, NATIONAL & YELLOW PAGES transfer sheet versions	£20-25
1023	1972	**AEC Single Decer Bus,** green, GREEN LINE transfer sheet	£20-25
1025	1971	**Ford Transit Van,** red, AVIS transfer sheet	£20-25
1027	1972	**Lunar Roving Vehicle,** blue & white paint	£20-25
1029	1971	**Ford D800 Tipping Truck,** green, yellow	£20-25
1030	1974	**Land Rover Breakdown Truck,** red or white	£20-25
1032	1975	**Army Land Rover,** green, transfers	£20-25
1033	1971	**US Army Jeep,** green, transfers	£20-25
1034	1975	**Mobile Gun,** green	£20-25
1035	1975	**Striker Anti Tank Vehicle,** green, transfers	£20-25
1036	1975	**Leopard Tank,** green, transfers	£20-25
1037	1974	**Chieftain Tank,** green, transfers	£20-25

1038	1975	**Scorpion Tank,** green, transfers	£20-25
1040	1971	**Sea King Helicopter,** white, orange or blue paint, transfers	£20-25
1041	1973	**Hawker Hurricane MkIIc,** green, white & blue paint, transfers	£35-40
1042	1971	**Spitfire MkII,** green/white/blue paint, transfers	£20-25
1043	1972	**SEPECAT Plane,** blue, transfers...	£20-25
1044	1972	**Messerschmitt BF109E,** brown, transfers	£50-60
1045	1975	**Panavia Multi Role Combat Aircraft,** green/white & blue paint, transfers	£20-25
1050	1975	**Motor Patrol Boat,** black, white & blue paint, transfers..	£10-15

ACCESSORY SETS

007	1960	**Petrol Pump Attendants** (35mm) plastic 2pce figure set. Clear plastic box, poly bag or yellow card box	£20
009	1962	**Service Station Staff** (35mm) 8pce plastic figure set. Clear plastic box, poly bag or yellow card box..	£25
13	1931	**HALLS DISTEMPER** hoarding with 2 carrying figures. Plain card box, printed end flap.......	£220
45	1935	**Garage.** Plain card box...	£420
46	1937	**Pavement Set.** Plain card box	£60
47	1935	**Road Signs 12pce set** (later renumbered 770). Yellow picture box...	£180
49	1935	**Petrol Pumps 5pce set** including PRATTS oil bin. Yellow picture box	£180
	1946	**Petrol Pumps 5pce set** (later renumbered 780) with plain oil bin. Yellow picture box	

The model pumps were based on real prototypes by Wayne, Bowser & Theo with the fourth based on one in use by Shell at the time. The Pratt's name was removed after WW2 as the company started to market the brand in Europe under the now familiar ESSO name

753	1962	**Police Controlled Crossing,** base with 2 keep left bollards, Policeman, black & white box & lamp standard. Yellow/red illustrated box	£90
754	1958	**Pavement Set.** Plain card box	£10
766	1959	**6pce British Road Signs** (country) Set (55mm) 1st type Yellow lift off lid box	£80
767	1959	**6pce British Road Signs** (country) Set (55mm) 2nd type Yellow lift off lid box	£80
768	1959	**6pce British Road Signs** (town) Set (55mm) 1st type. Yellow lift off lid box...............................	£80
769	1959	**6pce British Road Signs** (town) Set (55mm) 2nd type. Yellow lift off lid box..............................	£80
770	1950	**12pce Road Signs Set** (formerly set No.47). Yellow lift off lid box...	£100
771	1953	**12pce International Road Signs Set.** Yellow lift off lid box	£100
772	1959	**24pce British Road Signs Set;** 766, 767, 768 & 769. Yellow lift off lid box.................................	£155
780	1950	**5pce Petrol Pumps Set.** Picture box lid. US issue on FAO Schwarz, New York box sold for £200 ..	£140

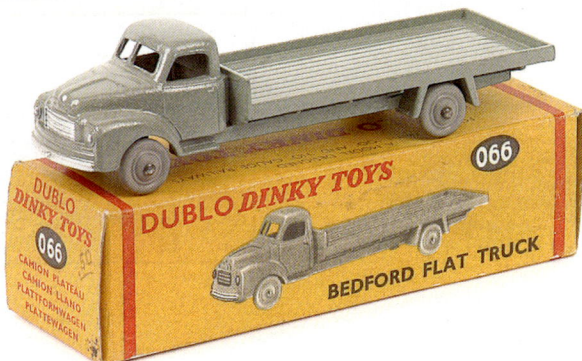

Dublo 066 Beford Flat Truck, grey version without hook.
Sold for £60 Toy Price Guide Archive. £200 has been paid for versions fitted with tow hook.

DUBLO

061	1958	**Ford Prefect,** fawn. Yellow illustrated box	£40
062	1958	**Singer Roadster,** yellow, red seats. Yellow illustrated box	£60
063	1958	**Commer Van,** blue. Yellow illustrated box	£30
064	1957	**Austin Lorry,** green, grey plastic wheels. Yellow illustrated box	
		Grey plastic wheels	£45
		Black plastic wheels	£70
065	1957	**Morris Pick-Up,** red. Yellow illustrated box	£50
		Dealers Trade Box containing 6 models. Sold in 2008	£360
066	1959	**Bedford Flat Truck** (no tow hook), grey. Plain red/yellow box	£60
		Rarer version with tow hook. Sold in 2009	£260
		Dealers Trade Box containing 6 models. Sold in 2009	£240
067	1959	**Taxi,** blue/white. Yellow illustrated box	£45
068	1959	**Royal Mail Van,** red. Yellow illustrated box	£65
		Dealers Trade Box containing 6 models. Sold in 2008	£460
069	1959	**Massey Ferguson Tractor,** blue. Plain red/yellow box	£30
070	1959	**AEC Mercury SHELL BP Tanker,** green cab, red back. Yellow illustrated box	£70
071	1960	**Volkswagen Delivery Van** (with windows), yellow. Plain red/yellow box	£80
072	1959	**Bedford Articulated truck,** yellow cab, red back. Yellow illustrated box	£40
073	1960	**Land Rover & Horse Trailer,** green & orange. Yellow illustrated box	£60
076	1960	**Lansing Bagnall Tractor & Trailer,** maroon with blue driver. Yellow illustrated box	£70
078	1960	**Lansing Bagnall Trailer.** Yellow illustrated box	£20
		Dealers Trade Box containing 6 models. Sold in 2010	£110

French 24L Vespa 400, light blue, metal ridged hubs, mint in nr mint yellow box.
Sold for £60 Toy Price Guide Archive

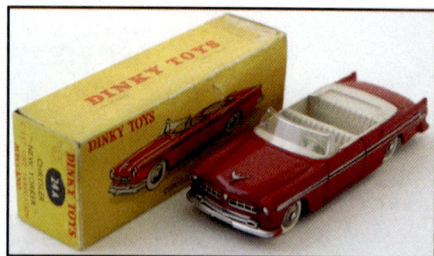

French 24a Chrysler New Yorker, dk red, silver trim, ivory interior, chrome spun hubs, mint in tape repaired box. Sold for £250 DJ Auctions

FRENCH DINKY

Ref.	First Issued	Model	TPG

CARS

22a	1933	**Roadster Sports,** 2-seater, all lead, grey version. Unboxed	£700
22A	1958	**Maserati Sport** (later renumbered 505), driver, dark red. Yellow illustrated box	£90
22b	1934	**Sports Coupe,** 2-seater, all lead, blue. Unboxed	£220
22c	1934	**Sports Roadster,** 2-seater, silver / red, white rubber tyres. Unboxed	£260
22d	1934	**Sports Coupe,** 2-seater, white rubber tyres. Unboxed	£230
23	1933	**Racing Car,** cast driver, coloured DUNLOP tyres matching paint flash, 4 exhaust pipes. Unboxed Blue, cream, orange & yellow versions	£80-100
23	1934	**Racing Car,** cast driver, black or white tyres matching paint flash, 4 exhaust pipes. unboxed Blue, cream, green, silver & white versions	£80-100
23a	1936	**Racing Car,** no driver, coloured DUNLOP tyres matching paint flash, 4 exhaust pipes. Unboxed Blue, cream, green, silver & white versions	£100-120
23a	1937	**Racing Car,** cast driver, cream, coloured DUNLOP tyres matching paint flash, 6 exhaust pipes. Unboxed	£150
23b	1935	**Streamlined Racing Car,** coloured DUNLOP tyres matching paint flash . Unboxed Cream & red versions	£170-200
23b	1937	**Streamlined Racing Car,** red, white DUNLOP tyres. Unboxed	£250
23b	-	**Hotchkiss Racing Car,** race numbers 1-6	
	1940	Red with metal wheels	£250
	1950	Red with black tyres	£140
23c	1949	**Mercedes Benz W154,** driver. Unboxed	
	-	Blue, rubber tyres	£70
	-	Silver, metal wheels	£180
23d	1951	**Auto-Union Record Car,** race no's 1 & 6. Unboxed	
		Light green, red hubs	£150
23H	1953	**Talbot Lago,** driver, race no's, blue. Yellow illustrated box	£60
		Trade box of 6 sold in 2008	£380

www.toypriceguide.co.uk

French 24B Berline 403 Peugeot, blue, metal ridged hubs, mint in an excellent yellow box. Sold for £140 Toy Price Guide Archive

French 24a Simca Chambord, white/red, chrome hubs, mint in excellent yellow box. Sold for £110 DJ Auctions

23J	1956	**Ferrari,** driver, red. Yellow illustrated box	
		Criss-cross grill version	£160
		Square grill version	£110
24A	1956	**Chrysler New Yorker** (later re-numbered 520), red & yellow versions. Yellow illustrated box	£90
24b	1934	**Limousine.** Unboxed	
		Green, grey & yellow versions with black/white DUNLOP tyres	£200-250
		Blue, green, grey, red & yellow versions with unpainted metal wheels	£180
24B	1956	**Peugeot 403 Berline** (later re-numbered 521), white tyres. Yellow illustrated box	
		Black	£150
		Blue	£90
		Grey	£80
		Yellow (or cream)	£120
24C	1956	**Citroen DS19,** open windows. Yellow illustrated box	£80-100
		Green	£100
		Ivory	£100
		Orange	£140
		Yellow	£60
24CP	1958	**Citroen DS19,** glazed windows. Yellow illustrated box	
		Green	£70
		Orange	£70
		Yellow	£170
24d	1934	**Vogue Saloon,** metal wheels, red. Unboxed	£180
24D	1957	**Plymouth Belvedere.** Yellow illustrated box	
		2-tone tan/brown	£260
		Fawn	£210
		Green	£70
		Grey	£100
		Trade box of 6 sold in 2007	£180
24e	1934	**Aerodynamic Saloon Car,** black/white DUNLOP tyres or painted metal wheels. Unboxed	
		Open chassis in blue, green, grey, red & yellow versions	£150-190
		Criss-cross chassis version with DUNLOP tyres, red. Sold in 2008	£420
24E	1957	**Renault Dauphine** (later re-numbered 524), open windows. Yellow illustrated box	
		Green, red & turquoise versions	£80
		Cream or ivory version	£260
		Scarce blue version. Sold in 2003	£420

French 24M VW Karmann Ghia, red with black roof, mint in nr mint yellow box. Sold for £80 Toy Price Guide Archive

French 549 Borward Isabella Coupe, light blue, metal dished hubs, mint in a tape damaged yellow box. Sold for £50 Toy Price Guide Archive

Ref.	First Issued	Model	TPG

24f 1934 — **Sportsman's Coupe,** black/white DUNLOP tyres or painted metal wheels. Unboxed
Green, grey, red & yellow versions £160-200
Blue, criss-cross chassis version with DUNLOP tyres. Sold in 2008..£340

24F 1958 — **Peugeot 403-U Familiale** (later re-numbered 525), open windows, light blue. Yellow
illustrated box £70
Rare dark red version produced for 1958 Meccano factory open day. Sold in 2005 ....£2,700

24g 1934 — **4-Seater Sports Car,** blue, cream, green, grey, red & yellow versions. Unboxed
With black or white DUNLOP tyres, wire screen £350
Metal wheel versions, tinplate windscreen £120

24h 1934 — **2-Seater Sports Car,** blue, green, grey, red & yellow versions, white DUNLOP tyres. U/b ..£200-250

24H 1958 — **Mercedes Benz 190SL** (later re-numbered 526), cream & silver versions with black roof. Yellow
illustrated box £80

24m 1948 — **Civilian Jeep,** red & military green versions. Unboxed £200-250

24M 1959 — **VW Karmann Ghia** (later re-numbered 530), red with black roof. Yellow illustrated box £70

24N - — **Citroeon 11BL,** black & grey vesions. Unboxed
1949 — 1st type casting with small rear window & spare wheel cover, black, metallic gold, metallic
grey & navy versions £150-200
1950 — 2nd type casting with wider rear window & spare wheel cover, black, metallic grey & metallic
gold versions £125-150
1953 — 3rd type casting, boot, large base plate lettering, black & grey versions 100-120
Trade box of 6 3rd types sold in 2009...£520

24O 1949 — **Studebaker State Commander.** Models supplied in trade boxes containing 6 models
Light blue, metal wheels...£190
Cream, metal wheels £640

24P 1949 — **Packard Super 8 Limousine**. Models supplied in trade boxes containing 6 models...........£600-700

24Q 1950 — **Ford Vedette,** grey, fawn, metallic blue & turquoise versions. Trade box of 6.....................£150-175
Rare green version sold in 2008 ....£320

24R 1951 — **Peugeot 203,** Metallic gold, grey, maroon. Unboxed...
Type 1 small rear window, smooth inside roof £100-130
Type 1, rare maroon version £220
Type 2 small rear window, cross hatched roof £75-100
Type 3 large rear window...£75-100
Type 3 rare blue version...£300
Trade box of 6 sold in 2007 ....£580

French 36B Willeme Aticulated Truck with tilt,
mint in torn blue/white stripe box.
Sold for £70 Toy Price Guide Archive

French 24Y Studebaker Commander, pale green
with dark green roof, VG in a creased box.
Sold for £120 Special Auction Services

24S	1952	**Simca 8 Sport** (later re-numbered 534), black, blue, gold, grey, green & Ivory versions. Unboxed	
		Thin windscreen version	£60-90
		Thick windscreen version	£100-130
		Trade box of 6 sold in 2008	£480
24T	1952	**Citroen 2CV,** grey & maroon versions. Unboxed	£65-85
		Later models in yellow illustrated box	£90-110
24U	1953	**Simca 9 Aronde,** blue, green & grey versions. Yellow illustrated box	£100-130
		* This was the first individually boxed French Dinky model	
24UT	1956	**Simca Aronde Taxi.** Unboxed	£75-100
		Trade box of 4 models sold in 2009	£200
24V	-	**Buick Roadmaster.** Yellow illustrated box	
	1954	Type 1 plain inner roof, blue version	£100-120
	-	Type 1 rare yellow version sold in 2008	£400
	1956	Type 2 crossed inner roof, blue & yellow versions	£150-200
	-	Type 2 rare pink version sold in 2008	£340
	-	Type 2 rare ivory version sold in 2008	£1,200
24X	1954	**Ford Vedette 54,** blue & grey versions. Yellow illustrated box	£90-110
24XT	1956	**Ford Vedette Taxi** (later re-numbered 539), black. Yellow illustrated box	£110-140
24Y	1955	**Studebaker Commander Coupe** (later re-numbered 537), light green, grey & orange versions.	
		Yellow illustrated box	£80-100
		Rare white (ivory), maroon roof & panels version. Sold in 2009	£300
		Rare orange, cream roof & panels version. Sold in 2009	£320
24Z	1956	**Simca Vedette Versailles,** light blue & yellow versions. Yellow illustrated box	£70-90
		Trade box containing 6 models. Sold in 2009	£260
24ZT	1959	**Simca Ariane Taxi** (later re-numbered 542), black	£90-110
30a	1935	**Chrysler Airflow,** blue, green & red versions. Unboxed	£140-180
		* Assembled in France	
35a	1939	**Simca 5,** black, blue, brown, gold, green maroon & yellow versions. Unboxed	£90-130
		Trade box of 6 mixed colours sold in 2010	£520
500	1967	**Citroen 2CV,** beige, blue/grey, grey. Yellow illustrated box	£60-80
		* Made in Spain (after 1974), included orange version, in pictorially illustrated box	£90-100
501	1967	**Citroen DS19 Police Car,** blue/white, roof light. Full artwork box	£170
503	1967	**Porsche Carrera 6,** white/red. Perspex display box	£70
		Trade box containing 6 models sold in 2006	£240

French 515 Ferrari 250GT, VG in excellent pictorial box. Sold for £75 Special Auction Services

French 531 Fiat 1200 Grande Vue, white with grey roof, mint boxed. Sold for £80 Toy Price Guide Archive

Ref.	First Issued	Model	TPG
505	1959	**Maserati Sport 2000** (formerly 22a), red. Yellow illustrated box	£70
506	1960	**Aston Martin,** green, race no's 1-17. UK made, yellow illustrated French box	£100
506	1967	**Ferrari 275 GTB,** red & yellow versions. Full artwork box	£70
507	1967	**Simca 1500 Estate,** grey & white versions. Full artwork box	£90
		Trade box of 6 sold in 2007	£380
507P	1967	**Simca 1500 Police Car,** white/blue. Sold in 2003	£5,200
508	1966	**Daf 33,** beige, bronze & red versions. Full artwork box	£70
		Trade pack of 6 (shrink wrapped) sold in 2009	£280
509	1966	**Fiat 850,** red, white & yellow versions. Full artwork box	£70
510	1959	**Talbot Lago** (formerly 23H), blue	£90-110
510	1965	**Peugeot 204**, beige, ivory & red versions. Full artwork box	£100
511	1959	**Ferrari** (formerly 23J), red. Yellow illustrated box	£140
511	1968	**Peugeot 204 Cabriolet,** light blue & red versions	£130
512	1962	**Leskokart Midjet Kart,** blue, plastic driver. Yellow illustrated box	£70
513	1966	**Opel Admiral,** metallic blue & metallic red versions. Full artwork box	£70
514	1966	**Alfa Romeo Giulia 1600TI,** grey, silver & white versions. Full artwork box	£110
515	1963	**Ferrari 250GT 2+2,** metallic blue & red versions. Full artwork box	£110
516	1964	**Mercedes Benz 230SL,** metallic grey, silver & red versions	£120
517	1962	**Renault R8** (later re-numbered 1517), blue, pale yellow & primrose yellow versions. Yellow illustrated box	£80
517P	1969	**Renault R8 Police Car,** blue/white promotional issue. Sold in 2010	£570
518	1961	**Renault R4L,** brown, blue, light blue & red versions. Yellow illustrated box	£80
	1964	Red POMPIERS de PARIS Fire Service promotional issue. Sold in 2007	£320
	1968	Yellow/blue PTT Post Service promotional issue	£200
		* Made in Spain blue version with PIRELLI tyres	£50
518A	1970	**Renault 4L AUTOROUTES,** orange complete with traffic sign pack (set 595r). Full artwork box	£220
519	1962	**Simca 1000,** light blue, grey & red versions. Yellow illustrated box	£60
		Light grey version	£240
		Dark red South African issue. Unboxed sold in 2000	£275

French 547 Panhard PL17, lilac, metal dished
hubs, excellent in a VG yellow box.
Sold for £80 Toy Price Guide Archive

French 545 De Soto Diplomat, dk pink/black,
silver flash, spun hubs, near mint boxed.
Sold for £120 DJ Auctions

520	1960	**Chrysler New Yorker,** metallic blue, red & yellow versions. Yellow illustrated box	£120
520	1963	**Fiat 600D** (later re-numbered 1520), cream, orange, ivory & red versions. Full artwork box	£80-100
521	1959	**Peugeot 405 8CV** (formerly 24B), cream & light grey versions. Yellow illustrated box	£70-100
522	-	**Citroen DS19** (formerly 24CP), orange & yellow versions. Yellow illustrated box	£150
523	1959	**Plymouth Belvedere** (see 24D)	-
523	1963	**Simca 1500** (later re-numbered 1523), light blue & metallic grey. Full artwork box	£60
524	1959	**Renault Dauphine** (with & without windows),brown, ivory, red & turquoise versions. Yellow illustrated box	£110-130
524	1964	**Coach Panhard 24CT**, grey & pale green versions Full artwork box	£90
		Double ended window box for export	£120
525	1959	**Peugeot 403 Estate,** sky blue. Yellow illustrated box	£80
525	1964	**Peugeot 404 Commercial Travellers Car,** cream, lt blue, dk blue & navy versions. Full artwork box	£80
		Red, POMPIERS de PARIS promotional. Sold in 2005	£1,250
526	1959	**Mercedes Benz 190SL** (formerly 24H), cream & silver versions. Yellow illustrated box	£80
526	1961	**Mercedes Benz 190SL Hard Top,** cream & silver versions. Yellow illustrated box	£80
527	1959	**Alfa Romeo 1900 Sprint,** blue & red versions. Yellow illustrated box	£80
		Rare turquoise version. Sold in 2007	£300
528	159	**Simca Vedette Chambord** (see 24K)	-
528	1966	**Peugeot 404 Cabriolet,** cream, metallic blue & white versions. Full artwork box	£130
529	1959	**Vespa 400 2CV** (formerly 24L), blue/grey roof. Yellow illustrated box	£80
		Orange/grey roof version	£200
530	1959	**VW Karmann Ghia** (see 24M)	-
530	1964	**Citroen DS19,** avocado green & red version. Artwork box	£130
		Silver version. Sold in 2002	£1,400
530	1976	Made in Spain version with plastic base	£90
531	1959	**Fiat 1200 Grande Vue** (formerly 24N), bronze/cream roof & ivory/blue roof versions. Yellow illustrated box	£70-90
532	1959	**Lincoln Premiere,** light blue & Metallic green versions. Yellow illustrated box	£90-110
		Silver version	£240
		Bright sky blue version. Sold in 2006	£520

French 537 Renault 16, metallic grey, mint
in a good illustrated box.
Sold for £50 Toy Price Guide Archive

Spanish made 538 Renault 16TX and 1413
Citroen Dyane, both mint in VG pictorial boxes.
Sold for £90 Toy Price Guide Archive

Ref.	First Issued	Model	TPG
533	1959	**Peugeot 203** (formerly 24R), cream. Yellow illustrated box	£80
533	1963	**Mercedes Benz 300SE,** blue, orange & red metallic versions. Detailed colour picture box	£70-80
534	1959	**Simca 8 Sport** (see 24S)	-
534	1963	**BMW 1500,** pale green & red versions. Detailed colour picture box	£80
		* Made in Spain metallic blue version with PIRELLI tyres	£350-400
535	1959	**Citroen 2CV,** blue, grey & maroon versions. Yellow illustrated box	£100
536	1959	**Simca Aronde Elsee** (see 24U)	-
536	1959	**Peugeot 404,** red, plastic trailer, roof rack with skis. Detailed colour picture box	£200
537	1959	**Simca Aronde Elysee Taxi** (see 24UT)	-
537	1965	**Renault R16,** light blue, sky blue & metallic grey versions. Detailed colour picture box	£70
		* Made in Spain bright blue version with PIRELLI tyres	£160-200
538	1959	**Buick Roadmaster** (see 24V)	-
538	1963	**Ford Taunus,** orange, red & turquoise versions. Detailed colour picture box	£80
538	1976	**Renault R16 TX,** metallic purple. Artwork box. *Made in Spain	£50
539	1959	**Ford Verdette Taxi** (see 24XT)	-
539	1963	**Citroen ID19 Estate,** metallic bronze & metallic gold versions. Detailed colour picture box	£90
540	1959	**Studebaker Commander** (formerly 24Y), orange, ivory & red versions. Yellow illustrated box	£90
		Orange with cream roof & cream lower panels version. Sold in 2009	£320
540	1963	**Opel Kadett** (later re-numbered 1540), green & red versions. Detailed colour picture box	£80
		Bright blue version. Sold in 2008	£200
541	1959	**Simca Vedette Versailles** (see 24Z)	-
542	1959	**Simca Ariane Taxi** (formerly 24ZT), black with red roof. Yellow illustrated box	£90
542	1964	**Opel Rekord,** blue, beige & grey metallic versions	£60-70
543	1960	**Renault Floride,** bronze, green & gold metallic versions. Yellow illustrated box	£80-100
		Ivory version. Sold in 2006	£520
544	1959	**Simca Aronde P60,** bronze/cream, grey & red/cream versions. Yellow illustrated box	£90
545	1960	**De Soto Diplomat,** pink/black roof & metallic green/cream roof versions. Yellow illustrated box	£80

French 542 Simca Ariane Taxi, black with red
roof, mint in nr mint yellow box.
Sold for £100 Toy Price Guide Archive

French 556 Citreon ID 19 Ambulance, light grey
with cream roof, metal dished hubs, mint in VG
yellow box. Sold for £100 Toy Price Guide Archive

546	1960	**Austin Healey 100-6,** white. Yellow illustrated box	£130
546	1964	**Opel Rekord Taxi,** black with red interior. Tellow illustrated box. *German export	£280
547	1960	**Panhard PL17,** lilac & orange versions. Yellow illustrated box	£70
548	1960	**Fiat 1800 Familiale Estate Car,** cream, lilac & yellow versions. Yellow illustrated box	£80
		Cream (yellow) version	£150
		Ivory, South African issue sold in 2008. Unboxed	£140
		Metallic green, South African issue sold in 2008. Yellow illustrated box	£480
549	1961	**Borgward Isabella TS,** grey, lt. Green & turquoise versions. Yellow illustrated box	£80
550	1961	**Chrysler Saratoga,** pink. Yellow illustrated box	£80
		Violet version	£130
551	1959	**Rolls Royce Silver Wraith,** 2-tone grey. Yellow illustrated box	£60
		Trade box containing 6 models sold in 2002	£420
551	1965	**Ford Taunus 17M Police Car,** green/white POLIZIE decal. Yellow illustrated box. *German export	£400
552	1961	**Chevrolet Corvair,** blue/grey, red & turquoise versions. Yellow illustrated box	£60
		Pale blue, South African issue. Yellow illustrated box sold in 2003	£600
		Pale grey South African issue. Yellow illustrated box sold in 2002	£400
		Smoke green, South African issue. Yellow illustrated box sold in 2002	£1,300
553	1961	**Peugeot 404,** light blue & white versions. Yellow illustrated box	£90
		Metallic grey, South African issue. Yellow illustrated box sold in 2008	£1,300
		Lime green, South African issue. Yellow illustrated box sold in 2002	£580
554	1961	**Opel Rekord,** beige, pink/cream roof & yellow/white roof versions. Yellow illustrated box	£70
		beige/cream roof & red/cream roof versions	£100
		Bright turquoise/ivory roof version. Yellow illustrated box. Sold in 2006	£640
		Bright blue South African issue. Unboxed sold in 2008	£580
		Metallic dark green South African issue. Unboxed sold in 2008	£580
555	1961	**Ford Thunderbird,** brown, red & white versions. Yellow illustrated box	£130
		Dark metallic blue South African issue. Unboxed sold in 2008	£580
556	1962	**Citroen ID19 Ambulance,** grey/cream roof. Yellow illustrated box	£110
557	1962	**Citroen Ami 6** (later re-numbered 1557), light blue & light green versions. Yellow illustrated box	£80
558	1962	**Citroen 2CV** (later re-numbered 1558), beige, green, grey & yellow versions. Yellow illustrated box	£80

French 570 Peugeot J7 ALLO-FRET Van, mint blue/white version in a VG pictorial box. The most common of the 3 known variations of for this model. Sold for £150 Toy Price Guide Archive

French 1410 Muskovitch, red, mint in a near mint pictorial box. Sold for £50 Toy Price Guide Archive

Ref.	First Issued	Model	TPG
558	1968	**Citroen 2CV,** 2-tone green & yellow / dark red versions ....£220-260 * Made in Spain	
559	1962	**Ford Taunus 17M,** metallic bronze, cream, grey, ivory, metallic grey / brown & white versions. Yellow illustrated box £70-90	
564	1969	**Caravelair Armagnac Caravan,** blue / white. Artwork box...£70	
565	1965	**Renault Estafette Camping Car,** lt. Blue / white roof. Detailed colour picture box £150	
811	1959	**Caravan,** beige or cream versions with white roof. Yellow illustrated box £50	
812	1965	**Camping Trailer,** luggage, cream £30	
1400	1967	**Peugeot 404 G7 Taxi,** black / red roof, G7 decal on rear doors. Detailed colour picture box £190	
1401	1967	**Alfa Romeo Guillia 1600Ti,** red, various race numbers. Detailed colour picture box..............£150	
1402	1968	**Ford Galaxie Sedan,** metallic beige, black, gold, maroon. & red versions. Perspex box .....£70-100 Black / white POLICE promotional. Sold in 2003 ....£1,250	
1403	1967	**Matra M530,** orange & white versions. Persex box..£45	
1404	1968	**Citroen ID19 Estate,** cameraman, grey / red, RADIO TEL LUXEMBOURG decal, camera man (camera in sealed paper bag). Detailed colour picture box £540	
1405	1968	**Opel Rekord,** metallic blue. Perspex box ....£70 Export version in double ended window box...£90	
1406	1968	**Renault 4L Sinpar 'Michel Tanguy',** 2 figures, green camouflage body. Detailed colour picture box, diorama tray & leaflet £280	
1407	1968	**Simca 1100,** metallic grey & silver vesions. Artwork box ....£50 Green version. Made in Spain...£60	
1408	1969	**Honda S800,** yellow. Artwork box...£80	
1409	1970	**Chrysler 180,** road sign, metallic blue & turquoise vesions. Artwork box £50	
1410	1968	**Moskovitch 408,** metallic bronze, metallic blue & red versions. Artwork box...............£70	
1411	1971	**Renault Alpine A310,** red. Artwork box £60	
1413	1968	**Citroen Dyane,** white, 2 plastic suitcases (sealed in bag). Detailed colour picture box. Also made in Spain £80	
1414	1969	**Renault R8 Gordini,** blue, race no. 36 decal. Artwork box...£130 Yellow promotional issue. Sold in 2005..£420	

French 1402 Ford Galaxie, metallic gold, good
condition within a damaged perspex box.
Sold for £100 Toy Price Guide Archive

French 540 Opel Kadett, ivory version with
dished metal hubs, VG in a VG pictorial box.
Sold for £125 Toy Price Guide Archive

1415	1969	**Peugeot 504,** light blue. Perspex box	£60
1416	1969	**Renault R6,** red & yellow versions. Artwork box. Made in Spain	£70
		Red, Fire Chief's Car, red Paris Fire Service logos.	£750
1417	1969	**Matra V12 F1,** driver, blue, race no. 17 decal, road sign. Artwork box with inner foam packing	£45
1419	1969	**Ford Thunderbird,** metallic green. Perspex box	£45
1420	1970	**Opel Commodore GS,** red/black roof & bonnet. Artwork box	£70
1421	1969	**Opel GT 1900,** blue, luggage rack. Detailed colour picture box	£80
1422	1969	**Ferrari 3L V12 F1,** driver, red, race no. 26, road sign. Artwork box	£45
1423	1969	**Peugeot 504 Convertible,** blue, road sign. Artwork box, inner packing ring & instructions	£160
1424	1969	**Renault R12,** mustard & yellow versions. Artwork box. Made in Spain	£60
		Blue Rally Car version	£90
1425	1969	**Matra 630 Le Mans,** blue & white versions. Perspex box	£40
1426	1969	**Alfa Romeo Carabo P33,** metallic green & yellow versions. Artwork box	£60
1428	1970	**Peugeot 304,** green & white versions, road sign. Artwork box	£80
1429	1970	**Peugeot Police Car,** white/blue POLICE decal, roof light. Artwork box	£160
1430	1970	**Fiat Abarth 2000,** orange. Perspex box	£45
1432	1970	**Ferrari 312P,** driver, red, race no. 60. Perspex box	£60
1433	1971	**Surtees TS5,** driver, red, race no. 14. Artwork box	£40
1435	1970	**Citroen Presidentielle,** driver, flag. Artwork box, moulded inner lid, card tray & leaflet	£320
		18" x 8" shop display poster for above model	£300
1450	1977	**Simca 1100 Police Car,** white/black. Artwork box. Also made in Spain	£50
1451	1978	**Renault R17TS,** orange. Artwork box. Made in Spain	£45
1452	1977	**Peugeot 504,** metallic bronze. Artwork box. Made in Spain	£45
1453	1977	**Renault R6,** blue/grey. Artwork box. Made in Spain	£45
1454	1978	**Matra Simca Bagheera S,** green. Artwork box. Made in Spain	£35
1455	1978	**Citroen CX Pallas,** metallic blue. Artwork box. Made in Spain	£45
1517	1964	**Renault R8** (see 517)	-

French 1432 Ferrari 312P with decal position sheet and road sign, mint perspex boxed. Sold for £65 Special Auction Services

French 1406 Renault Sinpar 4x4 with Michel Tanguy figure, mint boxed. Sold for £280 Toy Price Guide Archive

Ref.	First Issued	Model	TPG
1518	1964	**Renault R4L** (see 518)	-
1519	1964	**Simca 1000** (see 519)	-
1520	1964	**Fiat 600D** (see 520)	-
1523	1964	**Simca 1500** (see 523)	-
1539	1980	**VW Scirocco,** metallic green. Artwork box. Made in Spain. Made in Spain	£40
1540	1964	**Opel Kadett** (see 540)	-
1540	1980	**Renault R14,** metallic green. Made in Spain	£40
1541	1980	**Ford Fiesta,** metallic blue. . Artwork box. Made in Spain	£40
1542	1980	**Chrysler 1308GT,** metallic green. Artwork box. Made in Spain	£35
1543	1980	**Opel Ascona,** orange. Artwork box. Made in Spain	£45
1547	1964	**Panhard PL17** (see 547)	-
1552	1964	**Chevrolet Corvair** (see 552)	-
1553	1964	**Peugeot 404** (see 553)	-
1557	1964	**Citroen Ami 6** (see 557)	-
1558	1964	**Citroen 2CV Azam** (see 558)	-
1559	1964	**Ford Taunus 17M** (see 559)	-

GIFT SETS

24	-	**Passenger Cars Set** (6 cars consisting 24b, 24d, 24e, 24f & 24h)	
	1935	Yellow box version	£8-10000
	1936	Purple box version	£5-6000
	1940	Blue box version	£4-5000
24-55	1955	**TOURISME Touring Cars Gift Set** (5 cars consisting 24R, 24T, 24U, 24V & 24X). Blue/white striped box. Sold in 2009	£1,700
24-56	1955	**TOURISME Touring Cars Gift Set** (5 cars consisting 24R, 24T, 24U, 24V & 24Z). Blue/white striped box. Sold in 2006	£1,200

French 24F Peugeot 403 Familiale, light blue, metal ridged hubs, mint in excellent yellow box. Sold for £70 Toy Price Guide Archive

French 545 De Soto Diplomat, green with ivory roof, metal ridged hubs, mint in near mint box. Sold for £150 Toy Price Guide Archive

24-57	1957	**TOURISME Touring Cars Gift Set** (5 cars consisting 24A, 24B, 24E, 24Y & 24Z). Blue/white striped box. Sold in 2004 ....£1,500
24-58	1958	**TOURISME Touring Cars Gift Set** (5 cars consisting 24B, 24C, 24D, 24E & 24Z). Colour illustrated lid box. Sold in 2007 ....£950
500	1959	**Touring Cars Gift Set** (5 cars comprising 521, 522, 523, 524 & 541). Blue/white striped box. Sold in 2003...£1,400
503	1963	**Touring 'COFFRET CADEAU' Car Set** (comprising 5 cars 521, 522, 543, 544 & 545). Blue/grey box with press-our display. Sold in 2004 ....£950
536	1965	**Peugeot 404 & Trailer,** red car/cream trailer, roof rack with skis, luggage.........................£140-170
1460	1969	**Touring Cars 'COFFRET CADEAU' Gift Set** (6 model set comprising 501, 507, 508, 509, 513 & 514). Blue/yellow picture lid box. Sold in 2009 ....£2,300
1462	1969	**Three Days 'TROIS JOURS' Gift Set** (4 models comprising 507, 508, 509 & 514). Promotional set for Galleries Lafayette in Paris packaged in a SAC-CADEAU gift bag. Sold in 2008 ....£480

DINKY JUNIORS RANGE
Produced between 1963-69 as a budget range with fitted DUNLOP tyres

100	1963	**Renualt 4L,** green £120-150
101	1963	**Peugeot 404,** orange & red versions £120-150
102	1963	**Panhard PL17,** blue & grey versions £120-150
103	1964	**Renault R8,** red...£120-150
103	1969	**Renault R8S Gordini,** red...£120-150
104	1964	**Simca 1000,** light yellow & green versions...£120-150
105	1964	**Citroen 2CV,** grey £120-150
106	1965	**Opel Kadett,** yellow. Sold in 2007...£1,500

French 60C Super G Constellation Lockheed in AIR FRANCE livery, mint in a creased blue/white stripe box. Sold for £90 Toy Price Guide Archive

French pre-war 60D Breguet Corsaire Low Wing Monoplane, good condition with no fatique. Sold for £180 Toy Price Guide Archive

Ref.	First Issued	Model	TPG

AIRCRAFT

Ref.	First Issued	Model	TPG
60a	1935	**DeWoitine D388 Rainbow,** 3 propellers, cream/blue, gold/green & gold/red versions. Unboxed	£150-200
60A	1957	**Dassault Mystere IVa Jet,** grey. Yellow illustrated box	£30
60b	1935	**Potez 58,** single propeller, yellow/grey. Unboxed	£90
60B	1957	**Sud Aviation Vautour,** grey, SNCASO livery. Yellow illustrated box	£45
		Trade box containing 6 models sold in 2008	£190
60c	1935	**Henriot H180T,** single propeller, green. Unboxed	£110
60C	1956	**Super G Constellation Lockheed,** 4 propellers, silver, AIR FRANCE livery. Blue/white striped box	£70
60d	1935	**Breguet Corsaire,** single propeller,2-seater, red/green. Unboxed	£80
60D	1957	**Sikorsky S58 Helicopter** (also 802), white/grey/blue, SABENA livery. Yellow illustrated box	£60
60e	1935	**DeWoitine 500 Hunter,** single propeller, cream/green, red/cream & silver versions. Unboxed	£200
60E	1957	**Vickers Viscount** (also 803), white/grey/blue, AIR FRANCE livery. Yellow illustrated box	£50
60f	1935	**Cierva Autogiro,** with or without pilot, silver. Unboxed	£150
60F	1959	**Caravelle SE210** (also 891), grey/white/blue, AIR FRANCE livery. Blue/white striped box	£70
61a	1938	**Dewoitine D339 Rainbow L'Arc en Ciel,** 3 propellers, gold/blue. Unboxed	£400
61b	1938	**Potez 56,** 2 propellers, blue/silver. Unboxed	£120
61c	1938	**Farman F360,** single propeller, silver/yellow. Unboxed	£280
61d	1938	**Potez 58 Air Ambulance,** silver. Unboxed	£120
61e	1938	**Henriot H180M,** single propeller, silver. Unboxed	£80
61f	1938	**DeWoitine 500 Hunter,** single propeller, silver. Unboxed	£160
64a	1939	**Amiot 370,** 2 propellers, silver. Unboxed	£50
64b	1939	**Bloch 220,** 2 propellers, silver. Unboxed	£60
64c	1939	**Potez 63,** 2 propellers, silver. Unboxed sold in 2008	£580
64d	1939	**Potez 662,** 4 propellers, silver, F-ARAY reg. Unboxed	£90

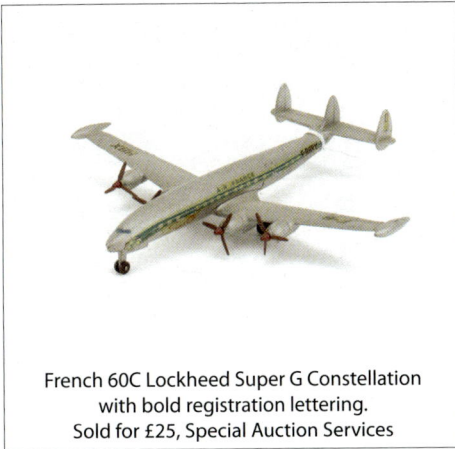

French 60C Lockheed Super G Constellation with bold registration lettering.
Sold for £25, Special Auction Services

French Dinky 60d Sikorsky S58 Helicopter. White and Blue. Mint in Mint box complete with inner packing. Sold for £60, DJ Auctions

800	1959	**Dassault Mystere IVa Jet** (see 60A)...	-
801	1959	**Dassault Mystere IVa Jet** (see 60B)	-
802	1959	**Sikorsky S58 Helicopter** (see 60D)..	-
803	1959	**Vickers Viscount** (seeo 60E)	-
804	1959	**Noratlas SNCAN**, 2 propellers, grey. Yellow illustrated box £140	
891	1959	**Caravelle SE210**, AIR FRANCE version, silver, F-BGNY reg. Blue/white striped box £90	
		AIR ALGERIE version. Sold in 2004 ....£520	
		SWISS AIR version. Sold in 2005...£360	
		SCANDINAVIAN AIRLINESERVICES version. Sold in 2004..£420	
892	1959	**Lockheed Super G Constellation** (see 60C)	-

GIFT SETS

60	-	**Aircraft Presentation Set** (6 models comprising 60a, 60b, 60c, 60d, 60e & 60f)	
	1935	Purple & gold box. Sold in 2003 ....£900	
	1937	Blue picture lid box (later re-numbered 501). Sold in 2007 ....£1,200	
60Z	1939	Green picture lid box AVIONS. Sold in 2005...£1,500	
60	1958	**COFFRET AVIONS Aircraft Presentation Set** (4 models comprising 60A, 60B, 60D & 60E). Blue/white illustrated lift-off lid box. Sold in 2003..£420	
61	-	**AVIONS Aircraft Presentation Set**	
	1938	4 model version comprising 61a, 61b, 61c, 61b & 61e within blue box. Sold in 2002 ....£600	
	1939	6 model version comprising 61a, 61b, 61c, 61b, 61e & 61f within green label box. Sold in 2009. £400	
64	1939	**AVIONS Aircraft Presentation Set,** 5 model version comprising 61a, 64a, 64b, 64c & 64d within green illustrated label box. £400	
501	1959	**Aircraft Presentation Set** (as set 60)	-

French 29E Autocar Isobloc, silver/red, ladder, red hubs, VG unboxed. Sold for £70 Wallis & Wallis

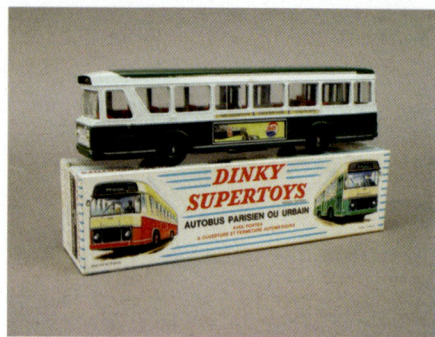

French 889 Autobus Parisien Ou Urbain, green/white, VG in a fair blue/white striped box. Sold for £80 Special Auction Services

Ref. First Issued Model			TPG

SHIPS

52c/ 52d	1937	**Normandie,** rollers, black/white/red. Blue picture label box	
		Plain inner	£80
		New York diorama inner	£150
53a/ 53b	1937	**Dunkerque,** rollers, grey. Blue picture label box.	£80
870	1962	**France,** white/black/red. Blue pictoral box with perspex inner	£80

GIFT SETS

50	1938	**British Naval Warships Set** (14 models comprising 50a, 50b x 2, 50c, 50d, 50e, 50f x 3, 50g, 50h x 3 & 50k). UK made in French box. Sold in 2007	£220

BUSES

29d	1939	**Renault TN4H Paris,** green/cream. Unboxed	
		Rubber tyre version	£180
		Metal wheel version	£120
29D	1952	**Somua Panhard Paris Bus** (also 570), green/cream. Yellow illustrated box	£90
29E	-	**Isobloc Autocar,** blue/silver, blue/cream, 2-tone green & red/silver versions. Unboxed	
	1950	1st type - smooth wings & smooth roof	£220
	1951	2nd type - moulded wings & smooth roof	£100
	1951	3rd type - moulded wings & ribbed roof	£70
29F	1956	**Chausson Autocar** (also 571), blue/cream & red/cream versions. Yellow illustrated box	£140
541	1963	**Mercedes Benz Autocar,** orange with white roof. Full artwork box	£70
570	1959	**Somua Paris Bus** (see 29D)	-
571	1959	**Autocar Chasson** (see 29F)	-
889	1965	**Berliet Autobus Parisien,** green/grey & red/cream versions, PEPSI & DUNLOP adverts.	
		Blue/white illustrated box, leaflet	£150
		Rare cream/green version. Sold in 2007	£2,300

French 24D Plymouth Belvedere, lt grey/red version, metal ridged hubs with white rubber tyres, mint in biro marked box.
Sold for £80 Toy Price Guide Archive

French 966 Marrel Bucket Unit, mint in VG box.
Sold for £95 Aston's

Example of a French 524/24E dual numbered box version of the Renault Dauphine, white with metal ridged hubs, VG in a good yellow box.
Sold for £160 Toy Price Guide Archive

French 24K Simca Verdette Chambord, cream/red, near mint in a good yellow box.
Sold for £70 Toy Price Guide Archive

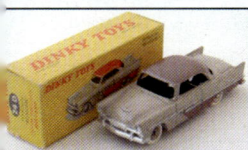

French 899 Delahaye Fire Escape, concave hubs, excellent in a VG box. Sold for £100 Toy Price Guide Archive

French 32E Berliet Fire Engine, red, silver ladder, white tyres, mint in an excellent blue/whuite stripe box. Sold for £120 Toy Price Guide Archive

Ref.	First Issued	Model	TPG

EMERGENCY

25D	1958	Citroen 2CV Fire Service Van, red, POMPIERS logo. Yellow illustrated box	£120
32D	1955	Delahaye Fire Escape (later re-numbered 899), red/silver ladder. Blue/white striped Supertoys box with instructions	£140
32E	1957	Berliet First Aid Fire Engine (later re-numbered 583), red, white tyres, silver ladder. Blue/white striped illustrated box	£140
80F	1959	Renault Military Ambulance (later re-numbered 820), green. Yellow illustrated box	£60
501	1967	Citroen DS19 Police Car, blue/white. Full artwork box	£200
507	1967	Simca 1500 Police Estate, silver & white versions. Full artwork box	£90
518	1964	Renault 4L, red, POMPIERS de PARIS logo. Promotional issue sold in 2007. Full artwork box	£320
525	1964	Peugeot 404 Fire Car, red, POMPIERS de PARIS logo. Promotional issue. Full artwork box	£300-340
551	1965	Ford Taunus Police Car, green/white, POLIZEI. German export. Yellow illustrated box. Sold in 2008	£400
556	1964	Citroen ID19 AMBULANCE MUNICIPALE, lt grey. Yellow illustrated box	£100
562	1959	Citroen 2CV Van, red, POMPIERS de PARIS logo. Yellow illustrated box	£110-130
566	1965	Citroen Currus Police Van, blue/white. Full artwork box with instruction leaflet	£200
568	1968	Berliet Turntable Ladder, red, extending silver ladder. Full artwork box with instruction leaflet.	£300
583	1959	Berliet First Aid Vehicle (see 32E)	-
820	1959	Renault Goelette Ambulance (formerly 80F). Yellow illustrated box	£50
899	1959	Delahaye Fire Escape (formerly 32D), red. Blue/white striped box, internal packinging piece.	£200
1416	1970	Renault R6 Fire Car, red, POMPIERS de PARIS logo promotional issue. Full artwork box sold in 2008	£750
1429	1970	Peugeot 404 Police Car, blue/white. Full artwork box	£160
1450	1977	Simca 1100 Police Car, black/white. Full artwork box, inner packing ring. Made in Spain	£50

FARM

27AC	1950	Massey Harris Tractor & Manure Spreader, red. Made in England, French picture box	£190

French 807 Ambulance Militaire, excellent in VG pictorial box. Sold for £100 Aston's

French No.14 Tiporteur with yellow hubs and grey driver, minor chipping. Sold for £135 Special Auction Services

LORRIES VANS & COMMERCIALS

14	-	**Triporteur** (3-wheel delivery vehicle), blue, grey, green, red & yellow versions. Unboxed	
	1935	Early smooth hub version (various colours)	£150-200
	1952	Later ridged hub version (various colours)	£100-150
		Trade box for 6 models containing one tan version. Sold in 2009	£540
14C	1950	**Coventry Climax Fork Lift,** orange/green. Made in England, orange French label box	£35
25a	-	**Open Lorry,** blue, brown, grey, green & red versions. Unboxed	
	1935	DUNLOP tyre version	£100-150
	1940	Metal wheel version	£60-100
25A	1950	**Ford Livestock Truck,** blue, grey & silver versions. Unboxed	£120-160
25b	-	**Covered Lorry, blue,** green, red & yellow versions. Unboxed	
	1935	DUNLOP tyre version	£180-240
	1940	Metal wheel version	£120-160
25B	1953	**Peugeot D3A Van,** green POSTES version. Yellow illustrated box	£90
	1953	Yellow/green LAMPE MAZDA version	£150
25c	-	**Flat Truck**	
	1935	DUNLOP tyres, turquoise/black, blue/red, green/black & red/brown versions	£160-200
	1940	Unpainted metal wheels, blue/black, cream/red, red/grey & green/black versions	£90-110

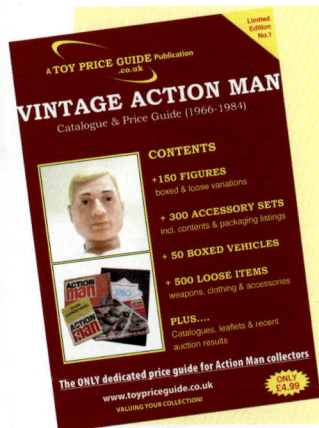

French 25D Tanker, 2nd version (1936-39), red without advertising, VG unboxed. Sold for £200 Wallis & Wallis

French 25BV Fourgon Postal Van, dark green with ridged hubs, mint in a VG yellow box. Sold for £80 Toy Price Guide Archive

Ref.	First Issued	Model	TPG
25C	1954	**Citroen 1200kg Van,** bronze/grey. Yellow illustrated box	£70
	-	With Louis Vitton label to base. Sold in 2009	£100
	1957	Cream/blue, GLACES GERVAIS logo version. Unboxed	£120
	-	Turquoise, CIBIE logo version. Unboxed	£45
25d	-	**Tanker Lorry,** red, ESSOLUBE or STANDARD decals. Unboxed	
	1935	Rubber tyre version	£100-150
	1940	Metal wheel version	£420
25e	-	**Tipping Lorry,** grey & red cab versions. Unboxed	
	1935	Type 1	£150-200
	1940	Type 2 open chassis	£100-120
25f	-	**Market Gardeners Lorry,** brown, cream, green or grey versions. Unboxed	
	1935	DUNLOP tyre version	£130-160
	1940	Metal wheel version	£50-75
25g	1935	**Flat Trailer,** metal wheels, blue, green, grey, red & turquoise versions. Unboxed	£25
25H	1949	**Ford Beverage Truck,** lt blue & red. Unboxed	£100-125
		Green version with tow hook. Sold in 2010	£260
25I	1949	**Ford Open Wagon,** blue, cream, grey, green & red versions	£120-160
25J	1949	**Ford Covered Wagon** red version. Unboxed	£140-170
		Blue SNCF version. Sold in 2008	£100
		Yellow CALBERSON version. Sold in 2010	£320
		Grey GRAND MOULINS de PARIS version. Sild in 2008	£100
25K	1949	**Studebaker Farm Produce Truck,** blue, green & red cab versions. Unboxed	£180-230
25L	1949	**Studebaker Covered Truck,** blue, red & turquoise cab versions	
		1st type casting	£250-300
		2nd type casting	£150-200
25M	1949	**Studebaker Tipping Truck,** dark green cab. Unboxed	£140-180
		Khaki version. Sold in 2008	£750
25M	1950	**Ford Tipping Truck,** green cab/grey tipper. Unboxed	£60-70
25O	1949	**Studebaker Milk Truck** (long bonnet), NESTLE logo,10 milk churns, blue/cream & blue/white versions. Red box, yellow insert card	£180-230
25O	1951	**Ford Milk Truck** (short bonnet), NESTLE logo, 10 milk churns, blue/white version. Red box, yellow insert	£275-325

French 33c Miroiter Simca Cargo Glaziers Truck, light grey cab, near mint in VG yellow box. Sold for £70 Toy Price Guide Archive

French 36A Willeme Log Carrier, mint complete with 6 log load in a damaged blue/white stripe box. Sold for £120 Toy Price Guide Archive

25P	-	**Studebaker Pick-Up,** green & yellow cab version. Unboxed £160-190
		Trade box of 6 sold in 2003 ....£950
25Q	1949	**Studebaker Covered Pick-Up,** green & yellow cab versions. Unboxed..............................£100-150
25R	1949	**Studebaker Breakdown Truck,** red, DINKY SERVICE logo. Unboxed...................................£110
25R	1954	**Ford Breakdown Truck,** red, DINKY SERVICE logo. Unboxed £200-250
25S	1949	**Single Axle Trailer,** red. Unboxed...£30
25T	1949	**Single Axle Covered Trailer,** red & yellow versions, tinplate canopy. Unboxed.........................£25
25U	-	**Ford Tanker,** red, ESSO logo. Unboxed
	1950	Version with hook & spare wheel support £175-225
	1951	Without hook & spare wheel support £60-70
25V	1950	**Ford Refuse Tipper,** dark green. Unboxed...£60
		Trade box of 6 sold in 2009 ....£220
30e	1936	**Breakdown Lorry,** DUNLOP rubber tyre & metal wheel versions in either blue, green or red. Unboxed...£275-350
32A	1952	**Panhard Articulated Lorry.** Unboxed
		Yellow KODAK version..£130
		Blue SNCF version £100
32C	1954	**Panhard Titan-Coder ESSO Tanker** (later re-numbered 576), red. Yellow illustrated box £110
33A	1955	**Simca Cargo Van,** green cab/yellow back. Yellow illustrated box...£100
		yellow cab BAILLY version...£150
33B	1955	**Simca Cargo Tipper Truck,** green cab. Yellow illustrated box..£80
33C	1955	**Simca Glazier'sTruck,** grey or yellow cab versions, MIROITIER SAINT GOBAIN logo.
		Yellow illustrated box £110-140
34B	1956	**Berliet Container Truck,** red cab. Yellow illustrated box..£70
35A	1955	**Citroen U23 Breakdown Truck,** red & dk red versions, DINKY TOYS logo. Yellow illustrated box..£100
36A	1956	**Willeme Log Truck** (later re-numbered 897), orange/yellow, 5 wooden logs. Blue/white striped box..£130
36B	1958	**Willeme Tractor & Closed Cab,** red/orange. Blue/white striped box..£120
38A	1957	**Unic Marrel Multi Skip Truck** (later re-numbered 895), grey/yellow. Blue/white striped box.£110
39A	1957	**Unic Boilot Car Transporter** (later re-numbered 894), silver/orange. Blue/white striped box with leaflet...£160

French 887 Air BP Tanker, white/yellow/green
in scarce pictorial top blue/white stripe box
with internal packing pieces.
Sold for £150 Toy Price Guide Archive

French 803 Unic Articulated Box Van in SNCF
livery with PAM PAM paper label, mint boxed.
Sold for £240 Toy Price Guide Archive

Ref.	First Issued	Model	TPG

39B 1959 — **Unic Sahara Pipe Transporter** (later re-numbered 893), beige cab, black pipe load. Blue/white striped box £100-120

70 1957 — **2-Axle Covered Trailer** (later re-numbered 810), red & yellow versions with tinplate canopy. Yellow illustrated box £35

560 1959 — **Peugeot POSTES Van,** green. Yellow illustrated box £90

560 1961 — **Fourgonnette Citroen 2CV Postal Van,** yellow. Full artwork box £170
Yellow PHILLIPS promotional. Sold in 2003 ....£650

561 1959 — **Citroen Van** (formerly 25CG) cream & white/blue versions. Yellow illustrated box
Cream GERVAIS logo version £140
blue, CIBIE logo version £220
Blue/white GERVAIS logo version £360
Blue BAROCLEM promotional, orange/blue illustrated box. Sold in 2003 ....£3,500

561 1972 — **Renault 4L Van,** yellow, PTT logo. Yellow illustrated box £260

562H 1965 — **Citroen 2CV WEGENWACHT Van,** yellow. Dutch export model sold in 2008.........£350

563 1960 — **Renault Estafette Pick-Up,** orange & green versions with green canopy. Yellow illustrated box £80

564 1963 — **Renault Estafette Mirror Truck,** Red, SAINT GOBAIN logo. Yellow illustrated box £120-150

565 1965 — **Renault Estafette Camper,** blue/white. Detailed colour picture box £150

567 1967 — **Unimog Snow Plough,** yellow/black. Detailed colour picture box...........................£110

569 1967 — **Berliet Stradair Side Tipper,** 2-tone green. Detailed colour picture box....................£190

570 1967 — **Peugeot J7 Taxi Van.** Detailed colour picture box
Blue/white & all blue versions with ALLO FRET logo £220
Blue/white, ICI logo. Sold in 2007 ....£650
Orange, AUTOROUTES logo. Sold in 2004 ....£360

571 1969 — **Saviem Goelette Horse Box & Sulky** (race horse, cart & driver), blue/white. Full artwork box with inner dorama tray..£440

575 1959 — **Panhard Articulated Lorry,** blue, SNCF logo. Yellow illustrated box..........................£280

576 1959 — **Panhard Titan Coder ESSO Tanker,** red. Yellow illustrated box £170

577 1959 — **Simca Cargo Van** (formerly 32AN), yellow/white, BAILLY DEMENAGEMENTS logo. Yellow illustrated box £170

577 1965 — **Berliet Livestock Truck,** 2 cows, yellow/green. Detailed colour picture box £160

French 895 Unic Boilot Car Transporter, mint in an excellent blue/white stripe box. Sold for £110 Toy Price Guide Archive

French 581 Berliet Truck & Container, red cab, silver back with grey load, mint in an excellent yellow box. Sold for £60 Toy Price Guide Archive

578	1959	**Simca Cargo Tipper Truck** (formerly 33B), green cab. Yellow illustrated box	£80
579	1959	**Simca Mirror Truck** (formerly 33C), grey & yellow cab versions. Detailed colour picture box	£130
581	1959	**Berliet Flat Truck & Container** (formerly 34B), red/black/grey. Yellow illustrated box	£60
582	1959	**Citroen Breakdown Truck** (formerly 34A), red, DINKY TOYS logo. Detailed colour picture box	£90
584	1961	**Berliet Covered Truck,** yellow cab with green canopy. Yellow illustrated box	£90
586	1961	**Citroen Milk Lorry,** 30 plastic milk crates, white/blue. Yellow/blue striped box	£340
587	1964	**Citroen PHILLIPS Display Van,** yellow/silver. Detailed colour picture box	£380
588	1964	**Berliet Beer Lorry,** barrels & crates, yellow/brown, BIERES LIMONADES, EAUX MINERALES logo. Detailed colour picture box	£200
		Red KRONENBOURG promotion. Sold in 2004	£2,800
589	1965	**Berliet Breakdown Lorry,** red & orange, DEPANNAGE logo. Detailed colour picture box	£200
596	1960	**LMV Road Sweeper,** cream/green. Yellow illustrated box	£60
597	1959	**Coventry Climax Fork Lift Truck** (formerly 14C), orange. UK made, French box	£40
803	1967	**Unic Articulated Lorry,** blue, SNCF & PAM-PAM logos. Detailed colour picture box	£260
805	1966	**Unic Multi Skip & Tanker,** red/black/white, PROPANE PRIMGAZ decal. Detailed colour picture box	£280
810	1959	**2 Axle Covered Trailer** (formely 70), red & yellow versions with green canopy, ESSO decal to some. Yellow pictoral box	£35
881	1969	**GMC PINDER Circus Truck & Trailer,** red/yellow/black. Full artwork box	£500
882	1969	**Peugeot 404 PINDER with Circus Caravan,** red/yellow/white. Full artwork box	£700
885	1966	**Saviem ' CAMION PORTE FER' Sinpar Steel Carrier,** red/grey. Detailed colour picture box	£300
887	1963	**Unic Articulated BP Tanker,** white/green/yellow, AIR BP decal. Detailed colour picture lid blue/white box	£160
893	1960	**UNIC Sahara Pipe Transporter** (formerly 39B), beige, 6 plastic pipes. Blue/white striped box	£100
894	1959	**UNIC Boilot Car Transporter** (formerly 39A), silver/orange, DINKY TOYS SERVICE LIVRAISON logo. Blue/white striped box	£130
895	1959	**UNIC Marrel Multi Body Truck** (formerly 38A), grey/yellow. Blue/white striped box	£110
896	1959	**Willeme Tractor & Trailer** (formerly 36B), red. Blue/white striped box	£130
897	1959	**Willeme Log Lorry** (formerly 36A), orange/yellow trailer. Blue/white striped box	£125

French 30/90A Roleau Compressor Richier, yellow, mint boxed. Sold for £90 Toy Price Guide Archive

French 885 Camion Saviem Porte-Fer, missing headlight & rusting, good box. Sold for £100 Aston's

Ref.	First Issued	Model	TPG
898	1961	**Berliet ALSTHOM Transformer Carrier,** orange, grey load. Blue/white striped box	£270
966	1961	**Marrel Bucket Unit Skip Lorry,** yellow with grey skip. Blue/white strped box	£150
1412	1968	**Hotchkiss Willy Recovery Jeep,** red/yellow. Full artwork box	£80
		Trade pack of 6 (shrink wrapped) sold in 2010	£320

GIFT SETS

25	-	**Commercial Vehicles 'CAMIONS LEGERS' Gift Set** (6 vehicles comprising 25a, 25b, 25c, 25d, 25e & 25f)	
	1935	Purple & gold box version. Sold in 2009	£2,100
	1940	Blue box versions. Sold in 2010	£700
25	-	**Commercial Vehicles Gift Set** (6 vehicles comprising 25h, 25i, 25j, 25k, 25l & 25m	
	1949	Blue box version. Sold in 2004	£3,400
	1949	Yellow box version. Sold in 2007	£3,200
	1950	Red box version. Sold in 2009	£3,100

CONSTRUCTION

34A	1955	**Berliet Quarry Truck,** blue cab/orange tipper. Yellow illustrated box	£80
		Standard issue in BERLIET Promotional box. Sold in 2004	£320
50	1957	**Salev Mobile Crane** (later re-numbered 595), grey/red. Yellow illustrated box with inner packing piece	£90
90A	1958	**Richier Rouleau Compresseur** (later re-numbered 830), yellow. Yellow illustrated lift-off lid box	£80
560	1958	**Muir Hill Dumper,** yellow. Made in England, blue French box	£45
561	1951	**Blaw Knox Bulldozer** (later re-numbered 885), seated driver, red. Made in England, blue French box	£80
562	1951	**Muir Hill Dumper,** yellow. Made in England, blue French box	£40
571	1951	**Coles Mobile Crane** (later re-numbered 972), yellow/black. UK made, blue French box	£60
572	1970	**Berliet 'BENNE CARRIERE BASCULANTE' Quarry Truck,** red/yellow tipper. Detailed colour picture box	£260
580	1959	**Berliet Quarry Truck** (formerly 34A), blue/black/orange. Yellow illustrated box	£100
585	1961	**Berliet Builders Lorry,** blue/orange/grey. Detailed colour picture box	£100

French 888 Berliet Sahara Crane Truck, minor
chipping in a pen marked box.
Sold for £120 Special Auction Services

French 818 Berliet Camion 6x6 Truck & Tilt, mint
boxed. Sold for £130 Toy Price Guide Archive

595	1959	**Salev Mobile Crane** (see 50).. -
830	1959	**Richier Diesel Roller** (formerly 90A), yellow. Yellow illustrated box £85
885	1959	**Blaw Knox Bulldozer.** Orange. UK made, French box £85
886	1960	**Richier Road Profiler,** yellow. Supertoys box £125
887	1959	**Muir Hill Dumper,** cream. UK made, assembled in France with French box £35
888	1960	**Berliet Sahara Pipe Layer,** tan. Blue/white striped box £140
		SOCIETE LANGUEDOCIENNE de FORAGES PETROLIERS promotional issue. Sold in 2004..£650
889	1959	**Coles Mobile Crane** (later re-numbered 972), orange/yellow. UK made, French box £55
972	1957	**Coles Mobile Crane** (formerly 889), orange/yellow. UK made, French box....................£55

MILITARY

24M	1946	**Military Jeep,** olive. Trade pack of 12 ....£150-200
80A	1957	**Panhard EBR75 FL11 8-Wheeled Truck** (later re-numbered 815), green. Yellow illustrated box£60
80B	1958	**Hotchkiss Willys Jeep,** (some with driver), green. Illustrated and non-illustrated yellow box versions £50
80C	1958	**AMX 13 Tank** (later re-numbered 817), green, rubber tracks. Yellow illustrated box £45
80D	1958	**Berliet 6x6 All Terrain Truck,** khaki. Illustrated and non-illustrated yellow box versions.........£60
80E	1958	**Obusier 155mm Gun,** green. Illustrated and non-illustrated yellow box versions £50
80F	1959	**Renault Goelette Ambulance,** green. Yellow illustrated box £50
676	1972	**Daimler Armoured Car,** green. UK made. Yellow/white illustrated box £150
800	1974	**Renault 4x4 Sinpar** (formerly 815), green. Yellow/white illustrated box £130
801	1973	**AMX Tank,** khaki. Yellow/white illustrated box £80
802	1974	**Obusier 155mm Cannon,** green. Yellow/white/camouflage illustrated box.............................£40
804	1973	**Mercedes Benz Unimog** (formerly 821), green, plastic canopy, net. Yellow/white/camouflage illustrated box £60
806	1973	**Berliet Recovery Truck** (formerly 826), green, net. Yellow/white/camouflage illustrated box£140
		Cream net version sold in 2005...£280
807	1973	**Renault Military Ambulance,** green. Yellow/white illustrated box £70
808	1972	**GMC US Army Recovery Truck,** olive green & sand versions. Yellow/white illustrated box £180

French 826 Berliet Military Crane Lorry,
mint in an excellent pictorial box.
Sold for £120 Toy Price Guide Archive

French 828 cellophane wrapped trade pack
of 6 Rocket Carrier Jeeps, mint.
Sold for £260 Toy Price Guide Archive

Ref.	First Issued	Model	TPG
809	1970	**GMC CAMION BACHE US Army 6x6 Truck,** driver, green, plastic canopy. Yellow/white illustrated box, card tray	£160
810	1972	**Dodge Command Car,** driver, green, net. Yellow/white/camouflage illustrated box	£80
		Trade pack of 6 (shrink wrapped) sold in 2010	£320
813	1969	**AMX with 155mm Gun,** green, grey rubber tracks. Full artwork box	£100
814	1963	**Panhard Armoured Car,** green. Yellow illustrated box	£40
815	1959	**Panhard EBR75 FL11,** green. Yellow illustrated box	£45
		Dual numbered yellow illustrated box	£60
815	1969	**Renault 4x4 Sinpar Gendarmarie** (later re-numbered 800), green. Yellow/white illustrated box	£110
816	1959	**Hotchkiss Willys Jeep** (formerly 80BP), driver, green. Yellow illustrated box	£40
816	1969	**Berliet Rocket Launcher,** khaki/grey, rocket. Yellow/white illustrated box, card tray	£110
817	1959	**AMX Tank** (formerly 80C), khaki. Yellow illustrated box	£40
818	1959	**Berliet 6x6 All Terrain Truck** (formerly 80D), khaki. Yellow illustrated box	£50
819	1959	**Obusier 155mm Gun** (formerly 80E), khaki. Yellow illustrated box	£40
820	1959	**Renault Goelette Ambulance** (formerly 80F), green. Yellow illustrated box	£50
821	1960	**Mercedes Benz Unimog** (later re-numbered 804), khaki. Yellow illustrated box	£45
822	1960	**White M3 Half Track,** green. Yellow illustrated box	£60
823	1962	**Marion Mobile Kitchen Trailer,** green. Yellow illustrated box	£45
823	1969	**GMC Military Tanker,** khaki/black. Yellow/white illustrated box	£260
824	1963	**Berliet Gazelle 6x6 Truck,** green. Yellow/white illustrated box	£80
825	1963	**GMC DUKW,** green, 4 drums & 2 crates. Yellow/white illustrated box	£90
826	1963	**Berliet Recovery Truck** (later re-numbered 806), driver, green. Yellow/white illustrated box	£130
827	1964	**Panhard EBR75 FL10** (formerly 815), khaki, metal hook. Full artwork box	£45
828	1964	**Jeep SS10 Missile Launcher,** driver, mounted launcher, green. Full artwork box	£60
		Trade pack of 6 (shrink wrapped) sold in 2008	£260
829	1964	**Jeep 106SR Gun Carrier,** driver, plastic gun, green. Full artwork box	£50
883	1964	**AMX Bridge Laying Tank,** green, folding plastic bridge sections. Full artwork box with instruction leaflet	£100

French 890 Berliet Tank Transporter with 80C
AMX Tank, both mint in a fair box.
Sold for £90 Toy Price Guide Archive

French No.21 Sujets en Miniature from 1938
all 4 pieces stamped 'Series Hornby' underneath,
VG condition in a repaired box.
Sold for £265 Special Auction Services

| 884 | 1961 | **Brockway Bridge Layer,** green, 10 plastic bridge components, 2 boats. Blue/white striped box, inner packaging & instructions ....£150 |
| 890 | 1959 | **TRACTEUR BERLIET Tank Transporter,** green. Illustrated & non-illustrates blue/white striped box..£110 |

RAILWAY

16	1935	**3-Car Railcar,** gold/red. Long scenic box £160
19a	1935	**Electric Locomotive,** blue. Unboxed £40
20a	1935	**Passenger Coach,** green & red versions. Unboxed £30
21a	1934	**Steam Tank locomotive,** green/blue. Unboxed £60
21b	1934	**Timber Wagon,** red/yellow metal log. Unboxed £40
21c	1934	**Coal Wagon,** green. Unboxed £40
21d	1934	**Crane Wagon,** blue. Unboxed £50
26	1934	**Bugatti Autorail,** cream/yellow, cream/green & all green versions. Unboxed £70

GIFT SETS

1	1934	**Station Staff Set** (6 figures). Plain lift-off lid box £120
2	1934	**VOYAGEURS Passenger Set** (6 figures & bench). Plain red lift-off lid box £320
3	1934	**Animals Set** (6 figures). Plain blue or red lift-off lid box £340
4	1934	**Railway Personnel Set** (6 figures). Plain lift-off lid box.........................£150
5	1934	**Railway Passengers Set** (6 figures). Plain red lift-off lid box £180
6	1934	**Shepherd Set** (6 figures). Plain lift-off lid box £240-280
10	1934	**Assorted Figure Set** (6 figures from sets 1,2 & 4). Plain lift-off lid box................£120-150
11	1934	**SUJETS Passenger Set** (5 figures). Red lift-off lid box £110
17	1935	**Electric Train Set** (contains 19a, 21b, 21c & 21d). Plain lift-off lid box..............£130-160
18	1934	**Steam Train Set** (contains 21a & 21c x 3) £140-180
19	1935	**Electric Passenger Train Set** (contains 19a & 20a x 3) £170-210
20	1935	**Steam Passenger Train Set** (contains 21a & 20a x 3) £150-180
21	1934	**Mixed Goods Steam Train Set** (tains 21a, 21b, 21c & 21d). Red box with internal dividers £260

Paper Dinky Toys shop display sign (23cm x 80cm) in after market frame. Sold for £100 DJ Auctions

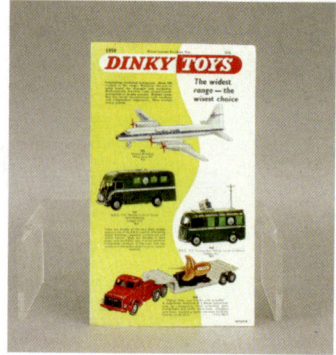

1959 Leaflet DT/CF/6 in mint condition. Sold for £20 Special Auction Services

Rare export issues of 271 Motorcycle Patrol; TS livery for the Belgian market and ANWB version for the Dutch market, both in VG unboxed condition. Sold for £120 Wallis & Wallis

South African issue 25b Army Covered Wagon (type 4), olive green, minor chipping, unboxed. Sold for £130 Wallis & Wallis

French 531 Fiat 1200, cream/lt blue, chrome ridged hubs, mint boxed. Sold for £110 DJ Auctions

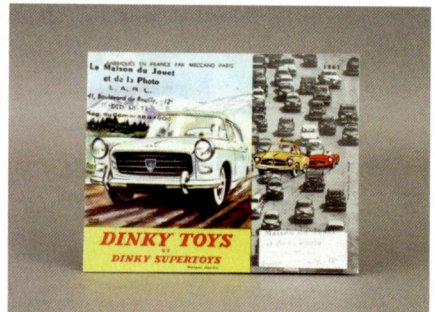

French 1963 catalogue in mint condition. Sold for £20 Special Auction Services